CRITICAL MENTORING

CRITICAL MENTORING

A Practical Guide

Torie Weiston-Serdan

Foreword by
Bernadette Sánchez

STERLING, VIRGINIA

COPYRIGHT © 2017 BY STYLUS
PUBLISHING, LLC.

Published by Stylus Publishing, LLC.
22883 Quicksilver Drive
Sterling, Virginia 20166-2102

Library of Congress Cataloging-in-Publication Data
Names: Weiston-Serdan, Torie, author.
Title: Critical mentoring: a practical guide/Torie Weiston-Serdan;
foreword by Bernadette Sánchez.
Description: First Edition. |
Sterling, Virginia: Stylus Publishing, LLC, [2017] |
Includes bibliographical references and index.
Identifiers: LCCN 2016034102 (print) |
LCCN 2016057444 (ebook) |
  ISBN 9781620365519 (cloth: acid free paper) |
  ISBN 9781620365526 (paperback: acid free paper) |
  ISBN 9781620365533 (library networkable e-edition) |
  ISBN 9781620365540 (consumer e-edition)
Subjects: LCSH: Mentoring in education–United States–
Handbooks, manuals, etc.
Classification: LCC LB1731.4. W39 2017 (print) |
LCC LB1731.4 (ebook) |
DDC 371.1020973–dc23
LC record available at https://lccn.loc.gov/2016034102

13-digit ISBN: 978-1-62036-551-9 (cloth)
13-digit ISBN: 978-1-62036-552-6 (paperback)
13-digit ISBN: 978-1-62036-553-3 (library networkable e-edition)
13-digit ISBN: 978-1-62036-554-0 (consumer e-edition)

Printed in the United States of America

All first editions printed on acid-free paper
that meets the American National Standards Institute
Z39-48 Standard.

Bulk Purchases

Quantity discounts are available for use in workshops and for
staff development.
Call 1-800-232-0223

First Edition, 2017

This book is dedicated to every young person who has shown me what it looks like to be free. The lessons you have taught me will not be forgotten—they will be passed on and inform the work of every mentor within my reach. Thank you for getting me #WOKE.

CONTENTS

A couple of years ago, I got an e-mail from an eager public school teacher from southern California who had read some of my work on race, ethnicity, and culture in youth mentoring. She wrote to tell me how she had been inspired by my writing and asked if we could talk on the phone because she wanted some advice and mentoring about her own professional development and writing. That e-mail was from Torie Weiston-Serdan, and little did I know how much she would inspire and influence me. She is pushing the boundaries in the youth mentoring field by introducing the idea of critical mentoring.

Traditionally, the field has taken a paternalistic and hierarchical approach to relationships between an adult and a young person; a wiser, more experienced adult provides guidance and support to the less experienced young person. Many of the youth who are served by mentoring programs are marginalized in various ways in our society because of, for example, their class, gender, race/ethnicity, or sexual orientation. Additionally, they may have faced serious problems or traumas in their lives that have caught the attention of adults (e.g., teachers) and are referred to programs that provide mentoring as part of their service delivery. The traditional approach to mentoring is focused just on the dyad and on what the mentor is providing to the youth; in some ways, it's a one-way relationship that doesn't consider what is happening outside of the mentoring interactions. In contrast, critical mentoring is an approach that puts youth themselves and their marginalization front and center and requires mentors and program staff to examine and address, *with youth,* the contextual and systemic forces that place these youth at the margin. Critical mentoring requires interacting with youth in a way that allows them to challenge the status quo. An example that Torie provides is respectability politics (Harris,

2014). Rather than mentors and program staff only teaching boys of color how to dress for success, they also have conversations that help them develop their critical consciousness around their dress. That is, they allow Black and Brown boys to question why wearing a hoodie makes them look suspicious when it is simply a fashion statement for White boys. These conversations aren't meant to scare boys of color or to disempower them, but instead to be aware of how White supremacy and racism play out in their everyday lives. These critical interactions among mentors and youth could plant the seed that allows young people to develop their own critical consciousness and leadership so that they engage their communities and society to change the status quo.

What is so inspiring about Torie's work is that she walks the walk. She lives and breathes critical mentoring. For example, as she got to know one of her protégés, he expressed the need for mentors to learn how to work with LGBTQQ (lesbian, gay, bisexual, transgender, queer, and questioning) youth. So the protégé and Torie codeveloped and cofacilitated a training curriculum for mentors working with this population. She talks about her own learning experience when working with her protégé. It's a two-way street, and the youth in her organization are front and center as they are partners and collaborators in the work that they do. Torie talks about putting her own assumptions and agenda aside, albeit sometimes difficult, to ensure that her organization's work is relevant to the youth they serve. What an empowering experience for youth! Her protégé must have felt so validated that Torie didn't just hear him, but together they took the next step, took action on his idea, and he was a leader in training development and implementation.

I write this in the wake of the Orlando shooting, where 49 victims lost their lives and 53 others were wounded, at a gay nightclub. Most of the victims were Latino young men. It was clear that this violent, hateful, terrorist act was the result of homophobia, heterosexism, and racism, at the very least. Mentoring as usual will not solve these deep-seated problems in our society. Focusing only on the mentor-youth relationship and interactions is obviously not enough. Some may say that this isn't the role of the youth mentoring field. I say it is. Critical mentoring challenges our field to question the status quo, to counter the negative and dehumanizing narratives about youth who are placed at the margins in our society, and to address the structural inequities they face. How can we empower program staff, mentors, and youth to face these problems head-on, to question these ideologies and perspectives, develop ideas about how to create social change, and then take action? Critical mentoring is the first step toward this change.

Bernadette Sánchez
DePaul University

ACKNOWLEDGMENTS

Thank you to my wife Dr. Gayle Weiston-Serdan for loving me, pushing me, and being mindful and respectful of the work I do. It is complicated, I know, to be a career woman of your own and still spend so much time contributing to and growing my career. I appreciate and love you.

Thank you to my mom, whose love, care, and pride in my work motivate me daily. I am the woman I am today because you modeled resilience, strength, and vulnerability all at the same time.

Thank you to my grandmother, whose unapologetic boldness lit a fire under me when I was very young. You taught me to speak my mind, no matter what. I'm proud to be a Torie.

Thank you to both my grandfathers, who always believed I was amazing and treated me as such. You both embody the father I never had, and I appreciate how consistently you have loved me.

Thank you to my Auntie Angie for being my first music teacher. You used hip-hop and R&B to teach me joy, love, respect, and understanding of myself. The older I get and the more I appreciate our music, the more I appreciate you for being the first to share it with me.

Thank you to my Brothers and Sisters for always having my back. Where my Dawgs at? I love you all so deeply.

Finally, to all those who have mentored and supported me through the years—Gracie Laudari, Dorothy Shamah, Bill Cook, Viv Ellis, Bernadette Sánchez, and Steve Vassor—I truly appreciate you and I hope this work makes you proud of me.

Thank you to Leah Heagy Alderete who shot the pictures of my protégés for the cover of this book.

INTRODUCTION

When I founded the Youth Mentoring Action Network in 2007, I had no idea what I was doing. I knew that my role as an educator was somehow different from the role I would play as a mentor, but I was not quite sure how. I knew that the one to one work in mentoring was necessary to help marginalized and minoritized youth build, but I was unsure about what "help" really meant. What I did know was that doing the work of decolonizing spaces, centering youth, and partnering with young people to pass on knowledge, reimagine structures, and create bridges to resources was only part of what I would do. I also knew that this would require a new kind of thinking, a new kind of action, one rooted in ancient tradition but remixed for new youth living in a new age. Critical mentoring is that remix. It is mentoring augmented by a critical consciousness, one that compels us to take collective action and to do it alongside our young people, hoping to move mentoring to another level and inspire youth in new ways. Critical mentoring is about helping youth to construct powerful identities and gain valuable work and school experiences that they can use in legitimate ways. Critical mentoring is the next juncture in mentoring practice—practice that challenges deficit-based notions of protégés, halts the force of protégé adaptation to dominant ideology, and engages in liberatory processes that trigger critical consciousness and an ongoing and joint struggle for transformation. It differs from mentoring as we currently know it, in that it moves beyond the dyadic structure of mentoring. Mentoring becomes much more about interrogating context and acting based on a critical analysis of that context, rather than an immotile relationship reinforced by hierarchy and saviorism.

My particular "brand" of mentoring, if you will, isn't necessarily grounded in ideas that I have developed in isolation; rather, they have come from my lived experiences and the lived experiences of the many protégés with whom I have had the honor of working. It is through open dialogue with my young people and through my willingness to decenter myself and other adults that I have come to many of the conclusions I present here. Much of what I posit in this book are merely lessons that my protégés have been gracious enough to teach me. The work I set out to do and the work my young people pushed me to do were two vastly different things. I, like many others, was not quite ready to examine my understanding of mentoring. And, I believe that we have yet to reimagine mentoring for the same reasons we have yet to reimagine other traditional institutions: power and control. Adults are still very much in charge, and that is what limits progress. Young people are naturally revolutionary, but adults tend to step in and alter their trajectories in ways that limit their potential. I had to learn, like many others will in the mentoring and youth development field, that mentoring is meant to be a collaborative partnership in which both mentor and protégé are intended to progress in critical ways. As these mentoring relationships progressed and my protégés taught me more, I began to develop a praxis termed *critical mentoring*. This approach is rooted in the premise that the mentoring process should be informed by critical theories so that it becomes a strategy capable of addressing the marginalization and minoritization of our young people. Critical mentoring requires a type of youth centrism that means young people have voice, power, and choice. It challenges hierarchical and age-old notions of the mentoring relationship, shifts the paradigm, and requires that we begin doing work that is participatory, emancipatory, and transformative.

This book is only a beginning. It includes a discussion of the critical mentoring concept, how it is informed by critical theories, especially critical race theory, and moves on to offer practical advice for making critical mentoring part and parcel of mentoring and youth development programs. As I address the micro of mentoring relationships and the macro of operating mentoring and youth development organizations, my goals are to help practitioners make sense of critical mentoring work on the ground, help researchers identify concepts on which to build, and help communities hold programs accountable. I end chapters 1 through 5 with a set of salient questions to ask and key actions to take. These are meant to move the reader from thought to action and provide a basis for discussion.

This book is meant to initiate a deep discussion about what mentoring is and what mentoring can be. It is intended to provoke critique and critical awareness and provide strategies that are immediately applicable. Because this text is a culmination of the lessons protégés have taught me thus far, it is most important that this be a text the young people who push me can be proud of.

I

THE ACT OF CLEARING THE
AIR AND PURIFYING THE
WATER

November 26, 2015: A 16-year-old Black boy being gunned down by police on the streets of Chicago is headline news. Before that, a Black girl being violently ripped from her desk, dragged across the floor, and handcuffed by a police officer in front of a classroom of young onlookers. This incident happens inside a public high school, but similar aggressions have been happening to marginalized youth across the country, with video evidence and plenty of social commentary. Before this young woman was assaulted in her classroom, a young man in California was attacked by police near a public bus stop. Before that, a woman in Texas who had been pulled over for a traffic violation and arrested was later mysteriously found dead in her jail cell. Before that, a young girl clad in a bathing suit who was attending a pool party was sat upon by a police officer. And so on. I do not say "and so on" with the intention of belittling the daily and state-sanctioned violence against Black and Brown bodies, but merely to abbreviate what would be a long and detailed list of such encounters. The physical violence is not a sole issue. There are also issues of economic oppression and suppression, calculated mis-education, and trauma in educational contexts; the school-to-prison pipeline; lack of culturally relevant spaces; and narrowly defined avenues of expression.

All of the examples I have mentioned vividly illustrate that minoritized and marginalized youth operate in contexts of racial, social, and economic toxicity. The words *minoritized* and *marginalized* are used to describe people who are othered in terms of mainstream ideologies and White supremacist ideals. They are folks whose identities have been racialized and problematized and whose status in society has been dramatically affected by this process. These two terms are used to encapsulate race, ethnicity, class, sexuality, gender, and ability. Marc Lamont Hill describes minoritized and marginalized folks as "nobody" in his most recent book. In fact, he notes the importance of recognizing the multiplicity of factors that contribute to this "nobodyness" and points very directly at the centrality that class has in creating "the material conditions and relations through which racism, sexism, and other forms of oppression are produced, sustained, and lived" (Lamont Hill, 2016, p. XX). This toxicity in which minoritized and marginalized youth exist stifles, humiliates, traumatizes, and kills. For mentors—and by *mentors* I mean adults dedicated to youth development work in which they foster long-term relationships dedicated to investing in young people and increasing their capacity for success—recognizing and addressing this toxicity is necessary. Youth context is important, but too often it is ignored in ways that can create transformative change. If the young people we mentor are operating in contexts like the ones I have described, then mentoring must address those contexts and do so in ways that challenge and transform. To borrow a metaphor from Steve Vassor, a nationally renowned mentor trainer, mentoring must move to "clear the water and purify the air" (Weiston-Serdan & Vassor, 2016). If young people's contexts were water and air, it would be impossible to breathe and impossible to drink. The critical mentoring process aims to address this. In other terms, critical mentoring attempts to address much larger systems that are complicated; overwhelming; and, frankly, "messy." It is not about using mentoring to manage symptoms, but leveraging mentoring to address root causes. The challenge for the mentoring world lies in its ability to partner with and support youth in their movements to purify the water and clear the air.

A Brief History of Mentoring

Before identifying ways to move mentoring into more critical spaces, it is necessary to look at what mentoring is, how it has evolved, and what critical work has been done to inform it. Rooted in an age-old concept and with its own complex and nuanced history, *youth mentoring* has evolved to become a popular and mainstream youth development strategy (DuBois & Karcher, 2014). Despite its ineffable nature, it is defined in the mentoring literature as a caring relationship focused on the consistent support and positive development of a child or youth (Keller, 2010). It has been studied to harness its empirical significance and impact (DuBois, Holloway, Valentine, & Cooper, 2002; Keller, 2010; Rhodes & DuBois, 2006). In fact, much of this research has helped the field of mentoring practice to expand as it illustrates a need for and the effect of mentoring relationships (DuBois et al., 2002; DuBois, Portillo, Rhodes, Silverthorn, & Valentine, 2011). More recently, the Obama administration has catapulted the idea of mentoring youth of color, especially young men and boys of color, into the mainstream with the My Brother's Keeper initiative (Rhodes, 2015; White House, 2014). Consequently, funding for mentoring programs, especially those serving marginalized youth, has swelled (Foundation Center, 2015). Because youth mentoring has a long and relatively positive social history, it is accepted widely and is said to "resonate with mainstream cultural values" (Keller, 2010, p. 23). The fact that it resonates so strongly with the mainstream may, in fact, be one of its problems, especially when it comes to the context of marginalized youth. And yet, programs clamor to serve these populations, namely because the private and public funding dedicated to these groups is widely available (Foundation Center, 2015).

The chronicled history of mentoring illustrates a compelling shift in ideas. Responding to the needs of urban America in the eighteenth century, mentoring reflected an attempt to inculcate White and middle-class values into youth who were the result of an increasingly industrialized America: poor and often unattended to (Baker & Maguire, 2005). However, these services were primarily focused on White youth. In 1904, the year Big Brothers of America was founded, racial segregation was the law and reality in the United States (Baker & Maguire, 2005).

Marian Wright Edelman (1999), a Black activist for children's rights, suggested that mentoring was alive and well in segregated America, but that minority youth were much more likely to be engaged in naturally occurring mentoring relationships. As it happens, the prominence of naturally occurring mentoring relationships in marginalized and minoritized communities is still very much the case. Though major mentoring programs may have found a newly racialized community to serve, at least according to statistics and funding trends, those communities still largely rely on their community-based networks to serve as mentors and, in effect, have managed to resist the colonization of their mentoring processes. The historical process of racialization is complex but necessary to understand. The fact that different populations have been racialized at various points and times in history is important to our understanding of how mentoring services have gone from catering primarily to poor and White immigrant communities to primarily poor, Black, and Brown communities (Roediger, 2006). Natural mentoring relationships happen outside of formal program structures; that is, relationships with extended family and close neighbors (Spencer, 2010). Though natural mentoring may have been and still is the way in which marginalized youth often engage in mentoring relationships, these relationships remain somewhat elusive in the mentoring world because they occur outside of the auspices of formal programs and are, as a result, challenging to quantify (DuBois et al., 2011; Hurd & Sellers, 2013). Studies focused on natural mentoring identify just as many benefits for these mentoring relationships as ones that happen in programs; namely, positive impacts on educational outcomes and protective factors against discrimination (Hurd & Sellers, 2013; Hurd, Sánchez, Zimmerman, & Caldwell, 2012). A lack of research on the ways in which natural mentoring occurs means that the processes still elude mentoring researchers and practitioners. Although social constructions have shifted to include non-White groups in mentoring processes, it is not to say that clear, critical, and culturally relevant ways of doing this work have emerged. It is apparent, given the history of mentoring, that it was not originally intended to serve those considered marginalized and minoritized by today's standards and that those communities addressed their mentoring needs outside of the formal structures available to poor Whites. This also means that mentoring, regarding its historical structure, is not prepared to do the work of clearing the air and purifying the water.

It was created to address not only deficit-based notions of youth but also systemic and institutional issues of race, ethnicity, class, sexuality, gender, or ability.

All of this brings us back to the notion of context; if the young people we mentor are operating in contexts like the ones described earlier in this chapter and the strategy we are utilizing was not meant to and does not address the context, then the strategy must be radically altered. Programs and the mentors recruited and trained by them claim to acknowledge problems in communities, but they fail to see that the problems are often more nuanced and complex than typical mentoring programs can handle. Instead, many of them focus on more manageable tasks such as improving student attendance, increasing grade point averages, and decreasing negative behaviors (Black, Grenard, Sussman, & Rorbach, 2010; M. T. Wang & Eccles, 2012). Although these outcomes are helpful, they do not address or help the youth to address the systemic and institutional challenges of race, class, gender, sexuality, ableism, and so on. They do, however, communicate to young people that assimilating to White and middle-class values will get them out of their communities, away from their contexts, and into spaces deemed more successful by program and mentor standards. In other words, mentors help young people adapt to toxic water and polluted air, rather than help them to purify the water and clear the air. The myriad of challenges facing marginalized youth require acknowledgment and the use of critical frames if mentoring is to be helpful.

assimilation > help.

A Conceptualization of Mentoring

The mentoring field has evolved since 1904 and strides have been made to define *mentoring* properly, establish standards for effectiveness, and create ways to conceptualize and measure mentoring processes and outcomes (DuBois & Karcher, 2014; Rhodes, 2015). In *Handbook of Youth Mentoring*, DuBois and Karcher (2014) illustrated a conceptualization of youth mentoring that highlighted five elements: activity, relationship, intervention, policy, and societal. The first two elements of the conceptualization focus primarily on relationships. Activity includes the social interactions mentors have with young people including the "guidance and other forms of support" (p. 4) provided. Relationship focuses on the "interpersonal ties" (p. 5) that prescribe the mentoring relationship as well as the "mentoring activity" (p. 5) that occurs. The latter part of the conceptualization (intervention, policy, and societal) moves beyond the one-to-one relationships and shifts to the language and actions of programs, communities, and governments. Intervention includes intentional efforts on the part of the mentoring program or agency to promote mentoring activities targeting specific groups and communities (p. 5). Policy is about government's providing meaningful support of mentoring in the form of initiatives and so on. Finally, societal seeks to promote positive perceptions of youth mentoring, to make youth mentoring more accessible and more attractive. DuBois and Karcher's conceptualization of youth mentoring makes a meaningful addition to the research and practice and provides solid definitions for the layers of work mentoring must do. I utilize their conceptualization because it is an essential research base for effective mentoring and articulates both the concrete and abstract work mentoring does. Although the conceptualization appears linear in nature, the authors describe it as "multilevel" because it begins with direct relationships and moves into more complex and nuanced efforts that include political and societal cooperation. However, DuBois and Karcher lay this out as an overview to be expanded upon in different areas, including the areas of "race, ethnicity and culture" (p. 5).

Race, Ethnicity, and Culture in Mentoring

In DuBois and Karcher's handbook, Sánchez, Cólon-Torres, Feuer, Roundfield, and Berardi (2014) develop foundational elements for dealing with race and ethnicity in mentoring relationships. They highlight four recommendations to consider in this work: racial similarity/dissimilarity, oppression, ethnic identity, and cultural competence. The racial similarity/dissimilarity component identifies several ways in which mentoring programs can adapt matching to preferences and needs. Sánchez and colleagues advocate for taking into account the preferences of protégés and their families when matching protégés to mentors. If protégés and families request matching according to a type of race, ethnicity, and culture preference, programs should accommodate. They also suggest that programs need to help mentors and protégés identify similarities in dimensions beyond race, ethnicity, and culture. Their proposal to intentionally provide same-race matches to youth who have few same-race models or who suffer from internalized racism is powerful and requires the mentoring program not only to be fully cognizant of race, ethnicity, and culture but also to understand it in complex and nuanced ways. Finally, they also advance that protégés who have limited exposure to people outside of their own race, ethnicity, and culture should have cross-race matches so that they can encounter other racial experiences. This suggests that not just racialized youth benefit from having mentors of color; White youth do as well.

For the element of oppression, Sánchez and colleagues (2014) suggest utilizing the Cultural Mistrust Inventory for adolescents to ascertain levels of cultural mistrust among the youth being served and to adjust "program support accordingly" (p. 153). They also posit that programs should create safe spaces for mentors and protégés to discuss racial prejudice, discrimination, and attitudes about racial and ethnic groups. In the area of ethnic identity, they recommend that programs assess their own knowledge and experience with ethnic identities to ascertain whether they are promoting healthy relationships between and among different racial groups. Furthermore, matching youth who have "weak ethnic identities" with those who have "strong ethnic identities" can positively alter the way youth see themselves, resulting in improved self-esteem and self-worth among youth being served (p. 153).

In their final recommendation, Sánchez and colleagues (2014) focus on the issue of cultural competence. They remind mentoring programs that both they and their mentors must be culturally competent and that to achieve that competence they must provide training around issues of race, culture, and ethnicity. Much of what the authors suggest about matching mentors and protégés along racial lines challenges a metanarrative in the mentoring literature about racial matching (Gaddis, 2012; Park, Yoon, & Crosby, 2016). An article by Park and colleagues (2016), which claims to test critical race theory (CRT), concludes that there are no "significant differences found in youth development based on racial/ethnic match" (p. 83). However, their study utilizes Big Brothers and Big Sisters of America data exclusively, which, as this chapter previously highlighted, has roots in segregated America, and never addresses their proclaimed use of CRT. More important, research that claims race does not matter in mentoring undermines the needs of those being served and knowingly or unknowingly functions as support for the colonization of culturally relevant mentoring practice. Again, critical frames are noted, but the analysis these critical frames require is conspicuously missing. The restrained ways in which the mentoring world currently addresses issues such as race make it necessary to utilize critical theories that will help us to understand youth context and identify processes for clearing the air and purifying the water. CRT, if utilized properly, is the start of that critical analysis.

Critical Race Theory

Initially born of legal scholarship, CRT "is a collection of activists and scholars interested in studying and transforming the relationship among race, racism, and power" (Delgado & Stefancic, 2012, p. 3). As a critical frame, CRT can provide powerful ways to reconstruct and enhance mentoring research and practice, especially as it looks to serve young people in marginalized communities. CRT rests on several core beliefs:

- Racism is an everyday part of life, part of the air we breathe and the water we drink, not random or unusual occurrences of blatant prejudice.
- Many civil rights or social justice victories are likely a result of something called *interest convergence*, the idea that White elite interests have converged with the requests of marginalized people.
- Race is a social construct, created out of "social thought and relations" (Delgado & Stefancic, 2012, p. 8), and different races, at various times and for various reasons convenient for society, are racialized.
- Discrimination is not linear in nature, and different aspects of an individual's identity can intersect to create more than one axis of discrimination. This concept is called *intersectionality* and is particularly helpful as mentoring and youth development professionals begin critically addressing

how the multiplicity of identities of the young people we serve are situated in society.

- The postmodern idea of challenging metanarratives is essential. Individuals who exist as marginalized beings have a unique perspective that can be expressed only by them. They call this process of storytelling *counternarrative* or *counterstorytelling*.

As a result of its intense reflections on race, racism, and marginalized identities, CRT provides ample opportunity to look at the mentoring experiences of and processes for mentoring marginalized youth. In fact, Gloria Ladson-Billings and William Tate (1995) establish CRT work in relationship to youth with their seminal article "Toward a Critical Race Theory of Education." CRT's work in education provides an even clearer base for the youth development world because much of our work deals with not only youth but also youth in relationship to educational contexts. Particularly important to connecting CRT to mentoring and youth development is the recent work of Adrienne Dixson. Her most recent piece utilizes a CRT frame to examine education reform, which is strikingly similar to the philanthropic processes that occur in the mentoring and youth development fields (Anderson & Dixson, 2016).

Furthermore, CRT does not operate solely in the American context. Scholars from the United Kingdom such as Nicola Rollock and David Gilborn utilize CRT in their educational research, studying the educational experiences of racialized populations in Britain and highlighting the global way in which race operates (Gillborn, Rollock, Vincent, & Ball, 2012). A new era of critical scholars has emerged as a result of CRT and these scholars have expounded upon the theory. For example, Michael Dumas (2016) writes about anti-Blackness in education and provides a solid base for a similar approach to interrogating the anti-Blackness in mentoring. Arash Daneshzadeh writes about youth incarceration and restorative justice and brings valuable insight into mentoring processes as they relate to youth struggling against prohibitive and anti-Black discipline structures (Daneshzadeh, Washington, & Cumi, in press). They, along with other "new critical scholars," make CRT a living and thriving theory that can be utilized as a concrete and illuminative framework for mentoring and youth development praxis.

CRT has either directly engaged in or provided a platform for pivotal conversations around issues of race, class, gender, and sexuality and other forms of othering. Mentoring researchers and practitioners need to better understand that problems facing marginalized and minoritized youth are rooted in pervasive, systemic, and institutional inequity and align those understandings with key components of mentoring processes, altering them to fully address the context of the youth they serve.

Critical Mentoring

As issues of inequity continue to persist within marginalized communities, the mentoring field must respond in ways that are at once transformative and emancipatory. Although some strides have been made, more critical notions of mentoring are in short supply. Sánchez and colleagues (2014) explained that

> despite evidence that race and ethnicity plays an important role in mentoring relationships, there are limited research-based guidelines in the practice field regarding how race/ethnicity should be considered. Some of the most important resources in the field, such as *Elements of Effective Practice* (National Mentoring Partnership, 2015) pay little attention to the role of race and ethnicity in mentoring programs. While the newest edition of the *Elements of Effective Practice* does include some discussion of race, it must also be noted that it is not in this particular tool kit's purview to produce an analysis of race in mentoring. It is simply a set of standards for the field. Recently, *Mentor* and *My Brother's Keeper,* recognizing a need for standards that address issues of race and ethnicity, released a special set of standards for the mentoring community. These standards focus on best practices that can be utilized when working with boys and young men of color (*Guide to mentoring boys and young men of color,* 2016) and the production of such a document signals a need for this type of work. (My Brother's Keeper, 2016)

As a direct response to Sánchez and colleagues' (2014) call to action for the mentoring field to better address issues of race and ethnicity, this book blends the most essential elements of mentoring research and practice taken from DuBois and Karcher's (2014) conceptualization with the most essential elements of CRT to inform a concept called *critical mentoring.*

Critical mentoring focuses on using essential components of critical theories, particularly CRT, to inform essential components of mentoring. Critical mentoring was developed to address the deficit that Sánchez and colleagues (2014) highlight (Weiston-Serdan, 2015; Weiston-Serdan & Vassor, 2016). Critical mentoring seeks to address a number of issues in mentoring that prevent it from being part of the solution that clears the air and purifies the water. Beginning with a critical understanding of the context youth exist in and then using basic components of CRT and other critical theories to inform mentoring activities, critical mentoring is the next level of mentoring research and practice, catapulting the work into a realm of activism and resistance. The components of CRT mentioned previously place marginalization front and center, making it necessary to understand context. Furthermore, beyond helping to understand context, these components lead us to viable actions for improving our programming in ways that speak directly to context. Mentoring work should follow, first understanding the complexities and nuances of marginalization and then explicitly moving forward to address and change them. For example, if the mentoring field first recognized that racism is normal in America, part of the water we drink and the air we breathe, it would also understand that program elements established to help young people avoid particular appearances or behave in respectable ways do not, in fact, offer young people innovative ways to survive or challenge racism. Instead, these elements actually serve to promote the existing structure of racism by teaching youth that assimilation to White and middle-class culture makes them more respectable and, therefore, less apt to suffer from racism. This concept is often referred to as *respectability politics* (Harris, 2014). We know for a fact that teaching our young protégés to dress and behave in certain ways, although possibly helpful for other reasons, will not protect them from racism that is structural, institutional, and normal. Instead, staff and mentors are trained to recognize the complexity of this issue, and program time is used to have discussions about concepts such as respectability politics. Rather than hold simplistic sessions around the need to "dress for success," hold sessions around the concept of respectability, including professional dress knowledge, and end with examples of attire that are appropriate for job and college interviews. In addition, the importance of always impressing upon young people that their attire is never an acceptable reason for them to be targeted, even if the world may see it that way, and having in-depth conversations about the White gaze and what it can mean for their safety is essential. Finally, encouraging mentors to follow up on these discussions with realistic pieces of everyday advice is also important.

CRT's concept of counternarrative or counterstorytelling also informs mentoring work. Mentoring often communicates via a metanarrative that is deficit based and adult centered. Scholar Richard Valencia explores deficit-based thinking at great length. Valencia (2010) describes *deficit thinking* as the idea that youth who fail, particularly in schools, do so because of some inherent lack or deficiency in them rather than in the systems around them. The media message that mentoring communicates is often one in which the youth is in need, the mentor fulfills this need, and then the mentor is heralded as a hero. This metanarrative is problematic because it views the young person as powerless and in need of saving and the adult as powerful and fully equipped. It ignores the capital that youth bring and can even be a turnoff to youth who do not feel they need mentors to "save" them. Shifting that narrative to include youth voice and communicating collaboration and partnership in mentoring rather than youth need and adult saviorism challenges existing notions about what mentoring is and makes it more attractive for young people who avoid mentoring to avoid being further marginalized. If the story of mentoring is told as if it is an outsider's answer to problems that ail marginalized youth, those being served may reject it and turn instead to natural mentors who better understand their story and who do not make them feel as if they are lacking something. Goings powerfully illustrates the concept of counternarrative in his 2015 autoethnographic account. While he focuses on the experience of the Black male educator, he highlights a national call for Black male educators that rarely includes discussion with Black male educators themselves, and that does not consider what happens to them when they join the teaching profession (Goings, 2015). Similarly, the focus on mentoring marginalized youth without including the narratives of the youth being served is a problematic feature of contemporary mentoring work. The issue of counternarrative particularly informs the latter elements of the conceptualization of mentoring, as programs look to highlight the importance of the work for society and government and to attract human resources and funding dollars. Using CRT tenets to inform the concept of mentoring or critical mentoring is a powerful way to move the mentoring agenda forward. Utilizing critical mentoring to frame mentoring research and practice provides a theoretical foundation that addresses issues still somewhat taboo and untouched in the field and allows the field to further deepen research and practice within marginalized communities. Critical mentoring yields more extensive conversations about race, gender, class, sexuality, ableism, and so on and offers ways to address how these issues permeate our society, the context that the youth we serve engage with daily.

time for anything else?

Shifting to a Critical Mentoring Process

Mentoring processes as well as the ways in which mentoring and youth development organizations operate must transmute, almost entirely, in order to provide critical mentoring services. Rather than focus on more methodical matching strategies, organizations must give more consideration to the preference of protégés, placing their needs at the forefront. This also means mentoring and youth development organizations have to do a much better job of recruiting diversely in an effort to ensure that mentors are available for the young people they serve. While too many organizations spend time remonstrating, Diego Romero, of Big Brothers Big Sisters of New York City, is blazing a trail for mentoring and youth development organizations to follow. He works to engage affinity groups that provide a stream of diverse volunteers. His solution is innovative. He is working closely with the community to ensure that its protégés have diverse match options.

These changes aren't simple, but they are necessary when addressing root issues. Tommy McClam, of Open Buffalo, talks about ensuring that minoritized and marginalized youth have access to wraparound mentoring services in a hybrid of group and one-to-one mentoring processes. This strategy ensures that it is not the responsibility of one mentor to meet all of a protégés needs; rather, it is the priority of a diverse mentoring "village" to produce the necessary support system. These actions are examples of making mentoring work more critical, both in micro and macro terms, and provide a basis by which to begin addressing issues raised in this chapter.

Mentoring relationships have too much potential and power when it comes to changing educational, career, and life trajectories of youth to remain an untapped resource. Critical mentoring has to be used first, to examine the history of the mentoring field, noting the importance of whom it was originally meant to serve and also how contemporary ideas of mentoring have evolved, as have classifications of marginalization. This point must also inform our critique of programs that exist in these communities almost wholly because funding dollars, not mission, purpose, or intent, dictate that they be there. Doing critical mentoring work means transforming communities. Accessing funding dollars to create token programs that do little to address systemic and institutional problems is, therefore, no longer an acceptable way to do nonprofit business. Furthermore, the way mentoring is packaged must be significantly altered. Though the mentoring field has begun to change its messaging, the concept is often packaged as deficit based, with images of Whites as mentors offering their expertise to often Black or Latinx and, subsequently, more unfortunate youth. This deficit base "colors" the way researchers study mentoring, practitioners implement mentoring, and marginalized youth perceive and experience mentoring. This issue is exacerbated by the number of mentoring programs and amount of funding pouring into impoverished and urban settings, as if young people in other contexts do not require mentoring as much as these youth do. Although high-need areas do exist, this framing encourages us to forget that marginalized youth also exist in suburban, rural, middle-class, and even wealthy settings. Throughout this text I suggest ways that mentoring and youth development programs can center youth and build on the strengths that both they and their communities possess. Beyond deficit framing, these youth require more dynamic mentoring relationships, ones that move beyond a dyadic relationship and toward institutional agency or opportunity brokering. Institutional agents and opportunity brokers take supportive conversations a step further and tap their capital and the capital of the institutions they navigate on behalf of those who have fewer opportunities otherwise (Stanton-Salazar, 2011). While the initial relationship is essential to gain trust and to provide guidance, these youth require access to resources that can help them to gain the needed capital. Many of these issues are centered in race, class, gender, sexuality, and so forth and would not be fully considered without a concept like critical mentoring. Ultimately, it is about how the field moves forward with an opportunity to enhance and expand what it studies; how it is studied; and, finally, how it is practiced. Nonprofits must operate differently, uniquely, and innovatively. Critical mentoring demands that we engage young people in more culturally responsive ways. Hierarchical notions of mentoring practice will no longer do; youth must become collaborators and partners. Critical mentoring requires a type of youth centrism that means young people have voice, power, and choice. Programs must make room for them on boards, on program committees, on staff, as training facilitators, as program ambassadors, even as evaluators of the program. Young people *must* inform the work, especially when operating in marginalized communities.

Questions to Ask

- How can our mentoring or youth development program be or become more critical?
- Is our program's mentoring approach considerate of the diversity of our young people?
- How traditional is my program? Is that traditional approach comfortable or uncomfortable for those we serve?
- Do we have open conversations about race in my organization? If not, how can we make open discussions about race part of our culture?

Actions to Take

- *Finish reading this book.* If this is the first time you have critically explored these issues, it's likely you haven't really considered alternatives to how things are traditionally done. Examine the ideas in this text to see if they resonate with you.
- *Start talking.* Having conversations with youth, staff, and other people in the field will give you an opportunity to see how others are thinking and feeling in relationship to these issues. Notice that I listed youth first. If young people are the ones we serve, they should be the first ones with whom we have discussions. Always ask them to engage in open and honest conversations; young people can always be trusted to set us straight.

- *Read more about critical theories.* Understanding the fundamentals of critical theory, critical pedagogy, and CRT can be helpful in the analysis of your mentoring and youth development work. You don't have to become an expert, but reading texts such as Paulo Freire's (1970) *Pedagogy of the Oppressed* and op-ed articles like Chris Emdin's (2016b) "How Can White Teachers Do Better by Urban Kids of Color?" will help you to connect easily with critical theories because these authors apply them to educational contexts, which means they are working with the same population you are.

The mentoring world has a responsibility to support young people. That support comes in different forms, and until now those forms have been pretty well defined. The next level of mentoring work lies in critical mentoring, utilizing critical frameworks to inform mentoring research and processes to make the work culturally relevant and transformative. Without this next level of praxis, mentoring will remain inert and dyadic, it won't become the multifactorial and transformative process that young people need it to be, and it definitely won't be the driving force behind systemic and institutional change. Critical mentoring seeks to move the field into a place where it can begin to address the levels of racial, social, and economic toxicity that suffocates marginalized youth. Critical mentoring is what the field needs to join a movement focused on clearing the air and purifying the water so that young people can live.

2

YOUTH CENTRISM

Critical mentoring provides a foundation that allows for an explicit connection between critical theories. Critical theories that help us to understand the intricacies of marginalization and minoritization and to gauge the levels of toxicity in the water and air are joined with conceptual components of mentoring; research-based elements necessary to providing valuable and relationship-based services for young people. But critical mentoring operates best at the nexus of praxis. And praxis for most mentoring and youth development organizations begins with programming. Since praxis is how theory is applied in practical ways, it is particularly important for critical mentoring, which is about translating theory into action. Critical mentoring offers the fields of mentoring and youth development the ability to address strategically issues plaguing marginalized youth through the daily work they do. But the paradigm shift required means looking carefully at the ways in which we plan and implement programs. It has been said, "Nothing about us without us," and that statement is apropos for mentoring programs doing critical mentoring work. Understanding this is paramount for engaging in mentoring and youth development work that focuses on clearing the air and purifying the water. Concentering youth participatory action research (YPAR) as a model, this chapter focuses on creating or restructuring organizations and programs so that they become youth centric.

Becoming Youth Centric

It was 2007 when I started building what is now called the Youth Mentoring Action Network. It was developed as a small school-based program, called the African American Mentoring Program (AAMP). Sure that Black youth on my high school campus where I was teaching needed guidance, support with grades, and encouragement to attend college, I rounded up every Black adult on campus to support this endeavor. I believed that together we could form a network of support for these youth as they moved through the program. The goal was to mentor these young people, provide them with academic support, and help them to go on to college. We organized college tours; we held tutoring sessions; we held open-forum discussions—anything we thought would interest and encourage them. These youth were never asked what they wanted and were never included in the planning and implementation process. They were to be beneficiaries of the time, energy, and resources we benevolently provided. Then Senator Barack Obama was running for the office of president, and we utilized one of our after school sessions to discuss the election and what we, at least as adults, had concluded as being most important: the possibility of America having its first Black president. That discussion was one I would never forget and served as the inception of critical mentoring practice for both me and the program.

Cameron was a junior in high school. He was the epitome of cool: He had swag; he navigated the youth and adult world seamlessly; he was wise beyond his years. Students loved him; teachers were frustrated by him. Cameron was a bright light in our program; he participated fully, attending all of the meetings and connecting with me as his mentor on a regular basis. I was aware of Cameron's no-nonsense attitude, but our mutual respect for one another meant we maintained happily balanced interactions with minimal conflict. Cameron was very vocal during our discussion about the presidential election. The perfect combination of street smarts and "traditional" book smarts made him a formidable foe in the debate. He held the belief that Obama, like any other politician, would do what needed to be done to become president, and thus, he would not be exceptional in any way, not even because he was Black. This thinking frustrated the Black adults in the room, and they challenged him. They posited that the notion of even becoming the first Black president was to be celebrated and admired, that the symbolism in and of itself was the beacon of hope we had all been looking for. Cameron did not budge. He argued, and boldly, that color had very little to do with being president. "It doesn't matter if the man is green or purple," he said. "Him being Black doesn't move me; my life ain't gonna change 'cause he's in the White House. I'd rather vote knowing that the person in office might do something that will directly impact my life." His critique of American politics was keen, critical, and stinging. In fact, some of the ideas that Cameron argued that day have since been articulated by critical scholars such as Cornel West. The Black adults in the room were offended. One, in particular, a guidance counselor on campus and mentor in the program, was infuriated by what he deemed as Cameron's "arrogant and dismissive" attitude. He defaulted to the notion that Cameron's youth, inexperience, and lack of pride in self were the reasons Cameron cared little about this exciting candidate. Soon the two were in a shouting match, with Cameron defending his ideas and the guidance counselor angrily trying to force Cameron to yield to his. Neither of them could know that my observation of this incident was a catalyst for analysis and change. As a program coordinator, I had not just witnessed the notion of youth voice, but grasped it. Cameron was better able to articulate a more nuanced understanding of race and politics than every adult in the room, and that somehow made all of us uncomfortable—so much so that at least one of us was willing to defer to silencing and demeaning Cameron rather than to engaging him. It became apparent, then, that the premise of this program was faulty and that we had misunderstood our role and the role of the young people we were meant to serve. Cameron had clearly demonstrated that he did not need us in the way we all assumed and that he was more than capable of doing much of what we set out for the program to do. He also demonstrated our need to provide space for him in ways we had yet to imagine. When the program year ended the first order of business was to part ways with any of the adult participants who had difficulty centering youth voice and engaging youth in ways that were collaborative and mutually respectful. The second order of business was to ensure that the adults participating in the program were decentered in ways that allowed for youth voice, agency, and partnership in operating the program.

A Tradition of Youth Voice

Although it may seem like a radical notion, there is a tradition of youth voice, agency, and leadership in this country in relationship to social movements. Even contemporary movements have been made more progressive with young people at the helm. The Black civil rights movement of the 1960s, for example, is a case of youth leadership that transformed the age-old discourse and ushered in a new era of Black activism in America. Stokely Carmichael, first as leader of the Student Nonviolent Coordinating Committee (SNCC) and then as a member of the Black Panther Party, was essential to capturing and voicing the youth perspective of the Black struggle for rights. He was 19 and a freshman at Howard University when he participated in his first freedom ride and is now heralded as one of the foremost Black thinkers. Appropriately, he is often credited for his role in the popularity of the rallying cry "Black power." In a 1964 speech that he made to a crowd of onlookers in Greenwood, Mississippi, he began by proclaiming that he would "say a number of things that need to be said in this country" ("Stokely Carmichael Videos," n.d.). The words were simple enough, but they signal the reason youth voice is of particular importance. Youth will often say the very things that adults are too timid to say and do the things that adults are too afraid to do, and that is why our organizations need them. A year before Carmichael made the aforementioned "tell it all" declaration, the civil rights movement received a breakthrough with its Children's Crusade, a concerted effort to include school-aged children in the nonviolent struggle against southern segregation. The approach was controversial but a direct response to the fact that it was difficult to engage adults who were entrenched in the systems being challenged because they depended on their reputations for economic necessity. In essence, their access to jobs and housing would have been impeded by clear association with the movement, and they were fearful of losing what little they had. Young people filled the void and embarked upon a campaign to "fill the jails," bringing international attention to the civil rights struggle happening in Birmingham, Alabama.

A strong tradition of youth voice and involvement is deeply entrenched in powerful social movements, and that tradition is being carried forward by groups such as #BlackLivesMatter and the Black Youth Project. These groups are among the many youth-initiated groups that work tirelessly to usher in a new and even more progressive civil rights movement, attempting to finish what the civil rights movement that came before them failed to do. The #BlackLivesMatter movement was founded by three queer Black women in 2012 as a direct response to the acquittal of George Zimmerman for the murder of 17-year-old Trayvon Martin. In their words, #BlackLivesMatter is "rooted in the experiences of Black people in this country who actively resist our dehumanization, #BlackLivesMatter is a call to action and a response to the virulent anti-Black racism that permeates our society" ("About the Black Lives Matter Network," n.d.). True to contemporary youth movements, #BlackLivesMatter challenges not only anti-Black racism but also the erasure of the queer presence and the female presence in Black social movements, so that their work and critique is intersectional as well as progressive. The Black Youth Project 100 is an activist organization "of Black 18–35 year olds, dedicated to creating justice and freedom for all Black people" ("Who Are We?," n.d.). In connection with the Black Youth Project founded by Cathy Cohen in Chicago, which is focused on researching Black youth ages 18–35, the Black Youth Project 100 is the action-oriented arm of the organization. Cohen's work as a researcher, the basis of the organization, has been rooted in community participatory research. Both #BlackLivesMatter and the Black Youth Project are excellent examples of youth-initiated and youth-centric social movements, but it can also be argued that these organizations are illustrative of credible and actionable research projects done in conjunction with those they serve. They essentially work alongside youth and communities to study, document, and present pressing issues.

There was then and still is now considerable debate about how involved youth should be in the leadership of movements, but despite our unwillingness to accept them, they have and will continue to lead. While mentoring and youth development programs may not consider themselves social movements, the work of clearing the air and purifying the water makes it necessary to engage in ways we may not have before. We must consider the limited fashion in which we approach services for marginalized youth and expand our notions of youth involvement and partnership so that we can provide the services they require and help them to make the changes they want. Young people have shown us time and again that they are sound and substantial

what about the quiet ones?

partners and leaders; it is us who refuse to recognize them in that way and who default to deficit-based notions of operating. YPAR models full youth and community inclusion and partnership and mirrors in many ways the processes we utilize in the mentoring and youth development field.

Youth Participatory Action Research

The participatory way in which critical mentoring requires us to work necessitates alternative models. YPAR is one of those models. Stemming from participatory action research (PAR), a qualitative research method that objects to the notion that "theory resides in one place, and its implementation in another" (McTaggart, 2001, p. 266), youth partner alongside adults as researchers and program coordinators. PAR rests on a collectivist endeavor that engages both "participant" and "researcher" in a project that not only investigates a problem but also acts to solve it through implementing an agreed-upon strategy or program (McIntyre, 2008). The history of PAR is situated in the context of critical research conducted in places such as India, Colombia, and Peru, spaces where marginalized communities and researchers utilized PAR as a viable stratagem for change (McIntyre, 2008). It is not by accident that PAR has its origins in marginalized communities of color where voice and agency matter most and should not be by accident that mentoring and youth development programs look closely at the model for ways to operationalize the concept of critical mentoring.

YPAR centers young people in its endeavors to explore and address issues in schools, communities, and other contexts that youth inhabit. Mentoring is at the heart of the YPAR concept because they are engaged as researchers and can participate in projects from start to finish. The University of California, Los Angeles (UCLA) Council of Youth Research models some of the critical mentoring work that mentoring and youth development organizations must do. In *Doing Youth Participatory Action Research* (2015), Mirra, Garcia, and Morrell not only provide a theoretical and epistemological basis for YPAR but also share the stories of a council of students, researchers, and teachers who confront relevant educational issues plaguing youth both locally and nationally. Together they identify research problems, collect and analyze data, brainstorm and implement solutions, and present their research findings. For these authors, the process was a powerful way to engage youth in processes that had typically been reserved for adult researchers and also "enlisted those most impacted by social problems in acquiring and sharing the knowledge needed to develop possible solutions" (Mirra et al., 2015, p. 470). In the same way that these researchers collaborated with youth in the research council, so should mentoring and youth development programs enlist young people to partner with them in planning and implementing youth programs. In fact, the authors refer to "re-imagining the nature of teaching and learning in formal and informal educational spaces" (p. 222). Likewise, mentoring and youth development programs must reimagine mentoring spaces, services, relationships, and youth development goals. Mirra and colleagues refer to a pedagogy of relationships (i.e., mentoring) as an essential aspect of their process. After building a relationship, they move into asking research questions, choosing methodologies, and collecting and analyzing data; and, finally, producing and sharing research. Each element of the YPAR process has its own set of expectations and they also directly address the concern of adult involvement:

> Adults have a crucially important role to play in facilitating the research process; that, indeed, their active mentoring support actually bolsters youth agency. Setting young people off on a research project without access to the resources, knowledge, and relationships that adults can provide can do a disservice to YPAR by denying students the necessary tools to reap the full benefits of the process. (p. 39)

Ultimately, YPAR work does more than just include young people in relevant processes; it helps to support and develop the astute, critical, and thinking youth we claim to cultivate with mentoring. Finally, Mirra and colleagues (2015) recognized YPAR as a way to address "the educational opportunities to which all young people are entitled and the race and class based inequalities surrounding who actually receives those opportunities" (p. 346). Examining the work done with the UCLA Council of Youth Research provides us with several guideposts for the work of critical mentoring:

- Center youth voices within our organizational structures.
- Make youth collaborative partners in our work.
- Engage in practices that are reciprocal in nature, meaning our young people inform our work as much as we help to support and develop them.
- Work alongside our young people to engage in critical processes that ensure we all get and stay woke. (The term #*WOKE* is taken from a social media colloquialism turned hashtag that means to be critically aware and conscious.)

In examining real-world and research-based strategies, critical mentoring brings together an array of resources that can help the mentoring and youth development world address the marginalization and minoritization of youth.

Also worth noting is another PAR spin-off called street participatory action research. Yasser Arafat Payne uses street PAR to organize what he terms *Black and Brown street-oriented people* and engages them in research converging on issues impacting them most. For Payne, these people "are best poised to critically examine the intimate and structural experiences of a population that have usually been ignored or dismissed" (Bryant & Payne, 2013, p. 231). Both YPAR and street PAR serve the same function: to engage those being served by projects in processes that will benefit them, better inform the work being done, and generate plans for action.

Getting Out of Young People's Way

Critical mentoring requires a youth centrism many youth-serving institutions are not ready for. Including young people in real and honest ways means being open to addressing the needs they raise. Every mentoring and youth development program working with and within marginalized communities should take a look at its program planning and implementation processes. If these processes have not been developed or reworked in collaboration with the young people being served, they must be changed. Doing work with marginalized youth means making space for their voices and extending them meaningful opportunities to participate in building their own programming. Making young people the absolute center of all planning, activities, fund-raising, training, evaluating, and so on is necessary. Youth centrism seems apparent given the field we are in, but by the time boards, funders, partnerships, and daily business operations pile up, organizations are often less youth centric than they initially set out to be. Being youth centric means being explicit about partnering with young people to plan and implement programs as necessary. Centering young people in the work will likely uncover the very issues of race, class, and gender, among others, at the heart of critical mentoring. The more we hear from our young people, the harder it will be to ignore these issues. Addressing marginalization is a daunting task and sometimes reason for trepidation because most organizations doing mentoring work are nonprofits and depend on funder support. However, the risk of not dealing with these issues lies in making the organization unnecessary to those we serve and, as a result, putting us in competition with the organizations set up to address needs we won't.

I mentor at least three young people every year. Each year my protégés offer me and the organization valuable content for programming. Adan and I had been meeting as mentor and protégé for one year before discussing the need to support mentors with their capacity to serve LGBTQQ (lesbian, gay, bisexual, transgender, queer, and questioning) youth. Meeting regularly and based on an agenda that my protégé set, Adan and I talked about everything from his school performance to the complexity of his identity. As a mentor, I was certainly versed in program expectations; I knew that keeping Adan on track academically and supporting him in his endeavor to go to college were of primary concern for my program. However, I was also keenly aware that the need to build a relationship in order to most effectively support him was pivotal. When Adan came out to me, it was a relief for both of us because we had been avoiding the figurative "elephant in the room." I was attentive to his need for added encouragement and support. I listened to him carefully and expressed that the mentoring relationship was a safe space for him. After a while, Adan decided to talk about how he had benefited from having a mentor who understood his sexual identity and who supported his need to live it openly. He also conveyed genuine concern that other youth like him might not have been lucky enough to connect with mentors who were able to support them in the same ways. After some discussion, Adan suggested that we help mentors better understand how to support LGBTQQ youth. I was not at all surprised by his care and willingness to act. We continued the conversation, ultimately deciding to collaborate on a training curriculum. After I provided Adan with some resources, we talked about what should and shouldn't be covered and together wrote a training curriculum for mentors of LGBTQQ youth. But Adan wasn't quite done; he volunteered to cofacilitate the training alongside me. Since then, Adan and I have trained teachers, college students, social workers, police officers, and others involved in mentoring work to address the unique needs of LGBTQQ youth. In many ways, our mentoring training has enjoyed even more success because Adan participated in every step of the process. Many training participants have shared the importance of hearing from a young person who has had firsthand experience. Indeed, the fact that Adan's perspective dictated the curriculum of the training, the activities participants experienced, and aspects of the dialogue significantly enriched the training. Having his lived experiences accepted, centered, and leveraged to help others not only helped him but also created one of the most sought-after services provided by our organization. My experience with Adan illustrates an incentive for mentoring and youth development organizations to center youth voice and participation. Although incentive should not be required, it is paramount to note the reciprocal nature of the process.

Strategies

Going about the work of centering youth is necessary from the very beginning of the program planning and implementation phase. It may seem that centering youth will make programming more difficult, but, in fact, making young people part of what we do is quite simple and mutually beneficial.

Begin by taking stock: If you have already established your organization and it isn't very youth centric, then asking questions that get at the heart and soul of your work is the first phase. Sometimes asking the tough questions can cause upset among your board and staff, but if you frame the process as making a mentoring and youth development program as youth centric as possible it should make sense to stakeholders dedicated to doing that work. If it doesn't make sense, changing the culture of the organization must become a priority. The leadership it takes to do this task is a challenge in and of itself (leadership for critical mentoring is discussed at length in the final chapter). If you are building a mentoring or other youth development program now, then it will be much easier to establish a tone of youth centrism from the beginning.

Questions to Ask

- Is your mission youth centric?
- How can you include youth in carrying out the mission?
- What processes do you have set up that can be reimagined and restructured to include young people? Or, how will you set them up for new programs?
- Have your program goals been devised alongside youth?
- How can YPAR be utilized in designing/redesigning programs as well as in implementing them?
- What roles can young people play at each level of the organization?
- How can young people be included in facilitating pieces of training, organizing events, or handling the day-to-day business of the organization? How are they bought in? How are you bought in to including them?

Actions to Take

- *Establish youth positions on your board of directors.* While boards serve the primary function of governing and fund-raising and seem very much like "adult" activities, our young people will provide a fresh set of eyes and new ideas to this process. In my experience, bringing in young people who have been served by the program to sit on the board has been the lifeblood of my organization. They see the programming from the inside out and can articulate what works well and what does not from firsthand experience. Although they might not be able to raise the funds you want your board members to raise, what they bring regarding perspective is worth its weight in gold. These board positions should not be for show either; they must come with the same voting and committee responsibilities that other board members have. This process not only benefits the organization but also effectively produces what mentoring and youth development organizations claim to do in the first place: provide opportunities for young people to grow, learn about social issues as well as entrepreneurship and business, and gain important school and career skills.

Dedicate staff positions to youth. Many mentoring and youth development programs have staff positions established for youth. However, those that don't need to look closely at models for doing so. DeVone Boggan, neighborhood safety director of Richmond, California, did just this with his radical approach to eliminate gun violence in the city. Faced with the staggering task of addressing 45 gun-involved homicides in one year, he decided that engaging and centering those perpetrating the violence was the most viable option. He picked "the 50 people in Richmond most likely to shoot someone and to be shot themselves" and employed them to solve the problem that they had contributed to causing (Wolf, Del Prado Lippman, Glesmann, & Castro, 2015). Their efforts to reduce gun violence in the city were immensely successful. The programming reduced gun violence in the city of Richmond, caused a number of policy changes directly related to the issue of gun violence, and provided jobs and education for the fellows participating in the program. In fact, one of the most compelling aspects of the program is that the people being "served" are directly involved in ways that alter their life trajectories tremendously. This compelling case may be outside the mentoring and youth development purview, but the fact remains that giving those we serve positions in our organizations is a powerful way to include them in the work. They not only have an insight few of us bring but also engage their community of peers in ways that we can't. They are

indispensable as community liaisons, and most organizations
that have youth staff spend very little time recruiting youth into
their programming; the staff makeup speaks for itself.

- *Give youth the role of program evaluators.* One of the most
important roles that young people can play in mentoring and
youth development organizations is as an evaluator. The checks
and balances that having young eyes on our programming provides are unparalleled. Engaging not only the youth we serve but
also other young people can provide a valuable perspective on
what we think we are doing and what we are actually doing. All too
often I hear adults pontificate about the benefits of said program,
focusing on adult-centric metrics, goals, and expectations, only
to hear the beneficiaries express the very opposite. If it does not
work for those we serve, then no matter how shiny the program
is for adults, it doesn't work at all. Working in conjunction with
young people to establish a methodology for evaluation and data
collection and then working with them to analyze and discuss
the data provides information both parties can use to grow. In
doing so we are also acting out the work we claim to do by
providing young people with opportunities to learn about and
conduct these processes. Establish a process for including youth
in all evaluative aspects of the work being done. These internal
evaluations are also helpful when putting certain committees
together for external evaluations.

"Nothing about us without us" is the refrain for youth centrism. As
highlighted in this chapter, it is essential to center the experiences of
those we serve, especially when working with marginalized populations. PAR and YPAR are ideas rooted in critical research and are utilized to give agency where there is little. It can't be stressed enough that
in doing this work well we are truly engaging in moving mentoring
from the realm of a dyadic relationship to one of institutional agency.
While centering our young people we are very literally helping them to
construct powerful identities and gain valuable work and school experiences that they can use in legitimate ways (e.g., as volunteer and work
experience for college applications, job applications, and career applications). Critical mentoring work requires that we begin to transform

mentoring space—to reimagine and renegotiate the hierarchical terms of mentoring. Centering youth is the ideal way to accomplish this and, at the same time, immediately tackles the issues of marginalization we aim to address by turning our bureaucratic space upside down and inside out, and putting the power in the hands of our young people.

3

CULTURALLY RELEVANT
MENTORING PRACTICES

Centering youth voice, power, and choice is not detached from addressing issues of marginalization and minoritization. As previously described, shifting power and altering hierarchical notions of place and order within organizations serve as strategies to promote agency in spaces that are meant to be youth serving but not necessarily youth inclusive. Providing space and opportunities for young people to be their own agents, to navigate freely and to be able to facilitate their own processes, means that mentoring and youth development organizations taking this approach have already begun the efforts to decolonize spaces. However, becoming youth centric, although significant, is only a part of addressing race, class, gender, sexuality, and other aspects of identity that are used to marginalize and minoritize young people.

Discussions about race, class, gender, sexuality, and ability, which I pointedly refer to as marginalization and minoritization, continue to provoke contention. And it is precisely for that reason that these discussions should continue, but in meaningful ways that transform thinking and systems to achieve equity. That's hard to do. And that may be why many of the discussions taking place in the mentoring and youth development world about marginalization and minoritization have been largely avoided. The rise of My Brother's Keeper and the work of organizations such as the Campaign for Black Male Achievement have compelled the mentoring and youth development fields to take note and engage in the discourse. Still, we struggle when it comes to finding viable ways to confront these issues with praxis. Critical mentoring compels us to address these issues head-on and provides us with tools we can utilize to begin addressing these challenges.

Events in Ferguson, Baltimore, Chicago, and Texas that have gained national notoriety and shifted national discourse around race are only manifestations of systemic inequity plaguing the country and the world. Long before America's gaze, communities like these and the young people being raised in them were subsisting despite battling stifling educational systems, gentrified neighborhoods, and state-sanctioned police violence. The attention garnered interest from policymakers, funders, and nonprofit groups into the communities to "help" the youth. The focus has been, and rightly so, on providing support for the young people who are disadvantaged as a result of these problems, but the strategies have been limited in scope and have done very little to address in substantive ways systemic and institutional wrongs.

During the discussion period of a presentation I gave on critical mentoring, one program coordinator shared her story with the group. She described helping to build and participating in programming for mentoring men and boys of color in Florida. The program, like much of the work happening in the arena of men and boys of color, dealt mostly with Black men and boys. She spoke fondly of her young colleague who had worked so diligently to build the program. She described him as an energetic, loving, and vigorous man who was an excellent model for the young men and boys they were both working to mentor. Her eyes began to glisten as she shared with us that this colleague, after experiencing car problems and pulling over on the side of the road, had a confrontation with local police that resulted in his death. She shared her distrust surrounding the official narrative released, having known the victim so well and having seen no signs that he would ever provoke an action that would lead to him being killed. Her story was heartrending, but her final thoughts were even more so. She ended by telling us that although her colleague, a Black man, exhibited every moral quality society asked of him—he was kind, he was caring, he was responsible, he served his community—none of that saved him from falling victim to racially motivated state-sanctioned violence. As she choked back tears, she managed to ask, "Do you know how hard it is to mentor a group of Black boys, telling them that if they 'just do this or just do that' they can be successful? How can I look at them and preach hope? And how does my mentoring help the reality they see daily?" Her desperation was palpable, and her questions the very same ones so many mentoring and youth development folks, who want to engage in critical work, have asked. Drawing on both research and practice, the critical mentoring platform begins to answer these questions. By utilizing critical work in other youth-focused fields to inform mentoring and youth development, practitioners will start to unearth ways of thinking and strategies to implement that can dramatically affect our impact.

Culturally Relevant Practice

A central body of work for mentoring and youth development organizations to consider is culturally relevant pedagogy. Gloria Ladson-Billings, the mother of culturally relevant pedagogy, brought the term *culturally relevant* to prominence in the early 1990s. Her seminal work *The Dreamkeepers: Successful Teachers of African American Children* (Ladson-Billings, 1995b) gave us vivid illustrations of what good teaching meant for young people of color. These very same lessons can be used to inform mentoring and youth development work focused on this same group of youth. In Ladson-Billings's (1995a) article "But That's Just Good Teaching! The Case for Culturally Relevant Pedagogy," she highlights three distinct components: academic success, cultural competence, and critical consciousness. For academic success, she addresses the myriad ways we expect our young people to be engaged as technical as well as social and political thinkers. That our young people learn the skills required to function in schools, workplaces, and society is a goal shared by mentoring and other youth development professionals. In fact, much of mentoring is centered on academic progress, even when not in school-based programs, because we understand the importance of academic excellence.

The concept of cultural competence is one of the most important aspects of culturally relevant pedagogy for mentoring and youth development. Focusing on making cultural value explicit is necessary to this process. Ladson-Billings describes cultural competence as "utilizing students' culture as a vehicle for learning" (Ladson-Billings, 1995a, p. 161). Rather than seeing the culture of the young person you are working with as separate from the goals you are trying to achieve, centering his or her culture as part and parcel and leveraging it to be more valuable is preferred. It is important that mentors pay close attention to this element. All too often mentors see themselves as arbiters of culture, particularly when it comes to leveraging mentoring to achieve the goals of the program.

Finally, Ladson-Billings lists critical consciousness as the third element of culturally relevant pedagogy. The concept of critical consciousness has been loosely referred to in the mentoring world, but with little practice that can be fully utilized to effect change. When we look at critical consciousness as part of culturally relevant pedagogy and, subsequently, culturally relevant mentoring, we need to consider that achieving the goals of academic success and centering youth and the youth's culture mean very little if the strategies used to achieve these goals are implemented individually or in isolation. Although we may achieve some success, the fact that we have not leveraged those elements to help the young person engage in a larger critique of economic, social, and political issues means we have lost the long game. As Ladson-Billings (1995a) states in her article, "Students must develop a broader sociopolitical consciousness that allows them to critique the cultural norms, values, mores, and institutions that produce and maintain social inequities" (p. 162).

Culturally relevant pedagogy offers significant insight into our work as mentoring and youth development practitioners. If we are going to do critical work, then we must utilize this model to inform the way we work with young people in our community programs. Although we are not schools, we function as a primary support for the work being done in schools and should leverage that position to ensure that our young people are gaining the skills they need to thrive academically. This often means doing and teaching what schools will not and giving youth access to academic enrichment. While Ladson-Billings laid the foundation for the practice, it has since been built upon by critical scholars such as Django Paris and Chris Emdin. Paris (2012) posits that culturally relevant pedagogy should be positioned as culturally sustaining pedagogy providing for a continual and multitudinal practice that becomes wide and more inclusive in its approach. Emdin (2016a) invites us to remix it with his connections to hip-hop, churches, and barbershops as spaces that model both relevance and sustenance.

The cofounder of the Youth Mentoring Action Network, Gayle Serdan, is an accomplished musician and embodies in mentoring practice what Ladson-Billings (1995b) describes as culturally relevant pedagogy. Many of the young people signing up to become part of our program did so because they wanted to be mentored by someone who understood the ins and outs of the music business. Again, allowing ourselves to be led by youth need, we began to connect all of our aspiring musicians with Gayle as a mentor. That aspect of our work began to grow so much that we now have an arm of our program dedicated specifically to music mentoring. The lackluster music programs in schools were not fulfilling for many of the young people we serve. Furthermore, the music education that did exist gave them very few opportunities to connect what they learned about music to the various fields of work in the music industry. Gayle not only engaged in one-to-one mentoring relationships but also supported these protégés academically in the area of music. She provided private piano lessons; she taught them music theory and she helped them to prepare music portfolios for applications to college-level music programs. Some of her protégés have gone on to become well-known musicians who perform onstage, compose music for film, teach music in schools, or run their own studios. To the point, she helped these young people to become academically successful in music and supported their endeavors by providing them with academic enrichment opportunities outside of schools. She helped them to gain the skills necessary to do the work they wanted to do.

Gayle's fascination with electronic music in the form of synthesizers and sequencers led her to begin working on a STEM (science, technology, engineering, and mathematics) in Music project alongside four of her protégés. Another one of our popular programs, STEM in Music brings together the inner workings of sound (physics); music theory (math); and gadgets such as synthesizers, sequencers, and music-coding software (technology and engineering). Her protégés have now had a range of academic experiences that begin with learning music and music theory, move to creating and identifying sound waves and coding hip-hop songs, and end with building sequencers and synthesizers—all valuable academic and career skills that these young people would likely not receive outside of her culturally relevant mentorship. Working primarily with young people of color, she centered their culture and lived experiences in the music. She moved beyond the western European concert music being taught to them in schools and exposed them to blues and jazz, making relevant connections between those music genres and the hip-hop music most of her protégés listened to. Instead of teaching them theory based in classical music, she taught them theory using the Tupac or Drake songs they brought to her during their regular meetings. She helped them to see the value in their culture, and not just in the contemporary hip-hop culture they closely identified with, but in the blues and jazz culture, from which hip-hop descended. She helped them understand that their culture had historical roots, a traditional genealogy of which they were a part. I would even argue that those who used this information in their portfolios or auditions were successful because of this knowledge of self they ultimately developed.

Ultimately, Gayle's music mentoring helped to develop a critical consciousness. Using music to have critical conversations, both she and her protégés would study different forms of protest music and look carefully at how musicians and their music commented on and critiqued sociopolitical issues and became soundtracks for social movements. This also meant interrogating the historical context in which these musical pieces were written and performed and making connections between the then and the now. In doing this, she not only helped to cultivate a critical consciousness but also helped the young musicians see themselves as viable parts of social movements with substantial roles to play.

Gayle models what culturally relevant mentoring practice looks like. Her use of structured activities was culturally relevant as well as in line with solid mentoring practice. Most mentoring programs require a certain number of times or hours mentors and protégés must meet, but making the content of those meetings culturally relevant is typically up to the mentor. However, the way in which programs train mentors has a direct impact on their mentoring practice. Culturally relevant pedagogy offers a great deal to mentoring and youth development practice, but we still need to look closely at our work to ensure it gets at the root of inequity.

Systems, Not Symptoms

Critical mentoring requires that we dive deeper into the critical consciousness aspect of culturally relevant practice. We must, in collaboration with our young people, be part of bringing forward solutions to the problems we have noted. Much of the solution creation has to begin with our own systems. Mentoring is essential for youth development, but mentoring as we now know it must be transformed in ways that can help youth understand and address complex issues of race, class, gender, and sexuality. Critical mentoring is built on the notion that mentors are critical actors within communities and that they build relationships with young people to collaborate and partner with them to challenge the status quo, responding openly and honestly about systemic issues, while having the wherewithal to support youth in confronting them (i.e., critical consciousness).

Critical mentoring means that mentors act as opportunity brokers to help young people access resources and extend their networks in ways that will assist them to overcome the often daunting obstacles they face getting through school, into college, and a career, helping them focus on the means to transform their communities rather than abandon them. It also involves critiquing and working to change the very systems their youth must navigate. For example, mentoring work has been done on the issue of keeping young people from engaging in behaviors that result in schools having to discipline them. But most of that work is centered on normalized discipline codes that often problematize youth of color and disproportionately punish them as a result. Instead of working to alleviate the symptom, teaching young people to "behave" in ways deemed appropriate, mentors have the opportunity to study the school-to-prison pipeline issue with their protégés and engage in a critique of the system. If the mentoring work we engage in serves only to endorse policies that undermine the humanity of the marginalized and minoritized youth we serve, then we are treating symptoms, not systems.

In similar ways, the deficit approach to mentoring is part and parcel of our system, but must be challenged to make work critical. Deficit-based methods are particularly harmful to young people because they assume the young person is missing something needed to be successful. As highlighted in this book, our young people already have much of what they need, but adults have problems accessing or accepting that. The mentoring narrative around what mentoring is and how it operates must shift. It is no longer acceptable to pronounce that mentors are saviors of youth. In fact, most of us engaged in mentoring work often express how much mentoring relationships have positively impacted our lives and how little we knew before our young person took on the task of teaching us. Critical mentoring means approaching a mentoring relationship without notions of a deficit. Like a culturally relevant teacher, a culturally relevant mentor seeks to enhance or complement what youth already have and supports them in the ways that these young people need most. Mentoring and youth development professionals who wish to do work in this field must rid themselves of the notion that adults, especially those who are more privileged, have been given the responsibility of rescuing "wayward" youth. This established metanarrative is a harmful part of our mentoring systems, which often isolate the same youth we hope to serve.

Again, it's not enough to celebrate the progress our young people have made or how far they have come if our ideas about them were rooted in what they lacked to begin with. Looking carefully at the way we use language in mentoring is an important part of this process because our language is often a reflection of our perception. You may have noted that I have been referring to my mentees as protégés instead. I use the term *protégé* because *mentee* often connotes deficit, whereas *protégé* most often connotes apprentice or points to a relationship less hierarchical. One of the first orders of business when helping organizations to set up their mentoring programs is to look for and address deficit-based language. Our work follows our language. Most of us are familiar with *Pygmalion* (Shaw, 1913), a play about a professor of language who takes up the charge to "fix" a street girl and make her acceptable to polite society. Mentoring is not like the story of *Pygmalion*; it is not an opportunity for the privileged to engage in the deficit practice of fixing the wayward natives. In fact, I have strong reservations about working with people who possess this ideology and have had to turn volunteers and collaborative partners away because I refuse to subject the young people I care for to this kind of toxicity. However, I have found that recruiting and training in ways that are culturally relevant makes it easier to attract people who are willing to engage in critical work. Looking carefully at the ways mentoring and youth development work treat symptoms rather than change systems and shifting our work to bring about change to those systems is crucial to making the critical mentoring transition.

No More Colonial Settlers

One of the most valuable discussions happening around cultural relevance in mentoring has to do with who is doing the work of serving minoritized and marginalized youth. This discussion is useful because it raises important questions that have to be unpacked, reflected upon, and addressed in real and honest ways. In the mentoring and youth development field, there are major organizations with lots of capital and connections that base their work in minoritized and marginalized communities. However, there are also smaller, grassroots organizations that are doing work in the very same places. These competing entities often have different approaches and different core values that influence the way they do work. I believe that there is an opportunity for both to do good work in these communities, but mutual respect and acknowledgment must lead. Again, critical interrogation is necessary. In this chapter so much has been said about not only centering youth themselves but also centering their culture and tapping into the wealth of resilience and knowledge minoritized and marginalized young people and their communities already have. This also means shifting our nonprofit business models to do the very same thing, which requires a concerted effort to connect to the community in ways that value them, not displace them. When mentoring and other youth development power players enter marginalized and minoritized communities and commence doing work that is not rooted in community values and not based on community culture and knowledge, they take on a colonial settler approach. They undermine existing and grassroots programs that have valuable funds of knowledge in navigating their communities, connecting with youth, and working in ways that are both locally and culturally relevant. As we move in the direction of addressing systemic inequality with mentoring and youth development work, we must have open and honest discussions reconciling ways in which marginalization and minoritization play out in our work. We must also determine how this can be addressed in lasting and fundamental ways as we alter how we operate inside and alongside communities. If communities and the grassroots programs inside them feel as if we are displacing and working against them, the goals we seek to accomplish will be lost in the mire. This is particularly evident when larger, more mainstream organizations have trouble recruiting mentors and volunteers of color. Many have cited a lack of volunteerism in the community. However, it has been noted that not only giving and volunteerism are significant in marginalized and minoritized communities but also the community members often argue that they are, in fact, engaged in active mentoring processes. It's just that their processes happen outside of major programs and in the culturally relevant ways that they believe are important. The fact that men and women from communities that are minoritized and marginalized are mentoring in their own ways, in their own spaces, and outside of typical mentoring contexts seems to baffle large mentoring organizations. And although these organizations are at least becoming aware of the fact that other reliable mentoring processes are happening outside their purview, they have yet to find the most effective ways to work within a partnership without upsetting or undermining them. The mentoring field's focus on naturally occurring mentoring relationships is evidence that these processes are a challenge. This brings us back to the point made earlier regarding putting ourselves in the position to compete with the communities we wish to serve. If those communities don't see us as viable, necessary, or in tune with their needs, they will still engage in mentoring and youth development work, but they will do so without us, and our concerted efforts to produce real change will be lost.

Engaging in culturally relevant practice is another aspect of critical mentoring. Looking at models that help us to understand how we can focus on and leverage the wealth of the culture in marginalized and minoritized communities as well as looking internally at ways in which our systems of operation help problems to persist rather than at ways to solve them will be necessary to critical and viable work.

Questions to Ask

- How is or will my organization be positioned in the community? How do or will the community members we want to serve see us?

- How can my program ensure that the ways we communicate our mission and program goals focus on cultural wealth rather than deficit-based notions?
- How can my program recruit in a manner that attracts members of our community?
- How can my program make sure that staff, volunteers, and mentors engage in culturally relevant practices?
- Does or will my program listen to the needs of the community in which we are located? Do or will we focus on issues important to us or important to our community?

Actions to Take

- *Build community.* If you are doing work in a community, it is necessary to build relationships there—not just the ones you think will matter for your bottom line, but the ones that will inform your work. What programs already exist, what kind of work are they doing, and why is that work important to the community? Find ways to collaborate and build connections. Be mindful of taking the colonial settler approach; don't forget that people were in these communities doing the work before you got there and they still will be after you are gone.
- *Recruit mentors within the communities.* Most nonprofit organizations find it hard to turn down volunteers, but, rather than importing them from outside the community, find ways to engage folks that are right there. If you find that community members are reluctant, ask them why. Maybe the work you are doing or the way you are doing it is off-putting or culturally disconnected. Recruiting is a surefire way to see whether the community is with you.
- *Train your people.* Not everyone will walk through your doors with a firm understanding of why they need to engage in the work the way you do. Ensure that every person in your organization, beginning with your board of directors, is given training on cultural relevance and the need to have these conversations and to move these conversations to real and tangible efforts as well as results.

- *Partner with the community to take on issues that are relevant to them, not issues you believe are relevant to them.* The Thomas Mentor Leadership Academy (TMLA) in Durham, North Carolina, modeled its entire program on this notion. Before starting, TMLA leadership went out and spoke to parents of the population they wanted to serve. They asked them what they felt their children needed and built a mentoring model on the information they received. They had the full support of the community and are doing incredible work with Black boys in the region. Doing what communities need is essential for doing critical work because it centers their voices and becomes a collaborative endeavor.

Critical mentoring is about cultural relevance. As Ladson-Billings (1995a) lays out in her education work, mentoring must become a process in which we actively work to ensure that our young people are well educated and given the resources they need. Often, it is mentoring programs not schools that provide the best spaces for young people to explore skills and concepts, and because of our one-to-one or small-group advantage, the young people we work with can engage in opportunities that allow for academic growth. When working in communities that lack adequate resources, mentoring and youth development programs doing critical work must make providing resources a priority. If the schools in the communities being served have few or poor music education programs, STEM programs, and so forth, the mentoring program serving them should make these academic supports available. And this is beyond the notion of tutoring young people inside schools; this is about enrichment outside of and beyond what schools offer. Centering this academic enrichment in the culture of those being served is necessary. Again, do what schools do not. Work with young people to understand who they are and where they come from, and then use that information to build enrichment opportunities that mirror their experiences. If they are aspiring scientists, find learning opportunities within their communities that directly link to their aspirations and with folks who look like them, people who match them racially; ethnically; in terms of gender, class, and sexuality. Young people need to see themselves and their future selves. At the Youth Mentoring Action Network we bring in guest speakers and provide workshops of various sorts for the youth we serve. We not only center these events on the needs of our young people but also make deliberate choices about who our presenters are. In this way, we ensure that our young people have opportunities to sit down and learn from and work with experts in various fields who represent diverse races, ethnicities, genders, and sexualities. We explicitly work with folks within the community and who reflect the population we serve. Finally, making sure that all of these enrichment opportunities are connected to a wider and critical consciousness makes the work culturally relevant. Our youth are skill building, and that skill building is centered in their culture, but it is also a starting point for discussion and action regarding social inequity. We ask questions about why we don't see marketing executives of color though we know they exist. We ask why predominantly White institutions are predominantly White and discuss the perks and pitfalls of attending them. We encourage our young people to be the next generation of critical workers, to participate in the effort to clear the air and purify the water.

The desire to make mentoring and youth development work more culturally relevant is instrumental in making mentoring more critical. Without an authentic connection to the community, we all lose out on valuable relationships, opportunities for collaborative work, and the creation of pipelines that pave the way for systemic change. If we aren't speaking to and with our communities and if we aren't valuing what they bring, then we are engaging in the same antiquated processes we are trying to challenge.

4

THE INTERSECTIONALITY OF MENTORING

In my definitions of *marginalization* and *minoritization*, I include the concepts of sexual identity, sexuality, and gender identity. Much of the discussion thus far has highlighted racialized identities and class. Although critical mentoring is meant to be applied to all forms of marginalization, it is too easy to adopt it and use it in only one corner of oppression. One of my critiques of historical social movements is that they have been unidimensional in nature. My admiration of new and developing social movements, those engineered by young people, is that they are much more inclusive of the various intersections on which many of our marginalized identities lie. For that reason, this chapter focuses on lesbian, gay, bisexual, transgender, queer, and questioning (LGBTQQ) youth and the critical race theory concept of intersectionality that can help to inform a wide-reaching and comprehensive understanding of critical mentoring. It must be noted that LGBTQQ is a simplistic identifier and is also meant to include a range of identifiers from pansexual to gender nonconforming.

I have had the opportunity to mentor many different types of young people, each of them exposing me to new dimensions of understanding, critical praxis, and language. My work with LGBTQQ youth has been the apex of all these. It is the epitome of my work because it is through working with LGBTQQ youth, particularly those of color, that I have come to understand how imperative it is to ensure that intersectionality is part of mentoring praxis. Without the inclusion of intersectionality, our mentoring becomes singular, inflexible, and unable to address the myriad challenges facing youth who are marginalized and minoritized. As Bettina Love (in press) notes, "we must be able to queer the space" if critical work is to be done. Because the focus of critical mentoring is about addressing systems and not symptoms, understanding the complexity of identity and the myriad ways these identities are problematized and marginalized helps us to understand inequity in more global ways and connects the mentoring movements happening in different parts of the mentoring world.

While my organization, the Youth Mentoring Action Network, works primarily with Black and Latino youth with the goal of assisting underrepresented youth to gain access to higher education institutions, our youth centrism means we are accepting of any young person who wants to engage with us. That openness brought several LGBTQQ youth into our fold.

Intersectionality

The Youth Mentoring Action Network operates in a vast suburban region approximately 121 miles east of Los Angeles, California. It is the heart of a traditionally Republican and conservative area, which is important to note when it comes to dealing with LGBTQQ issues that are often considered controversial and taboo. While the region is one of the fastest growing areas in California, it is experiencing a demographic shift, with increasing numbers of Blacks and Latinos migrating from large urban areas (i.e., Los Angeles) to suburban areas. It follows a national trend noted in the research of Robert Teranishi in 2005. There are several high schools in the area, all attempting to deal with the demographic shift in terms of school culture and academic statistics. None of them are doing a very good job of it. We have all seen very public evidence of the inane ways schools have been handling racial disruptions, disproportionate statistics for students of color, and daily instances of blatant homoantagonism on campuses all over the country. Because these issues are teeming with controversy, most schools elect to avoid them, at least in direct and calculable ways. LGBTQQ youth have not always been welcomed into traditional schooling spaces and have had to struggle for some of the basic rights heterosexual youth already enjoy. In some schools rainbow shirts, the rainbow being symbolic of gay pride, have been banned. In other schools, charters granted to groups of students who want to have student clubs have been denied for LGBTQQ students who wish to gather. LGBTQQ youth also have regular encounters with bullying from both students and staff. Additionally, the suburbs lack community youth centers, so the principal places to hang out are schools and shopping malls. All of these details are essential to understanding our work with LGBTQQ youth; as discussed previously, context matters. Also, note that race and class are still included in the discussion.

While this chapter focuses on LGBTQQ youth, they don't exist on an island and including them forces us to have conversations about how all of these issues intersect. It is in this context that I had my first experience mentoring queer youth, particularly four queer men of color. While I have worked with queer women and transgendered youth, I center queer, cisgender men in this conversation particularly because these four young men were crucial to my development as a critical mentor and because they helped me to discover a more nuanced understanding of mentoring in relationship to the complex identities of young people. My centering them is also meant to be a critique and call to action for the My Brother's Keeper mentoring work, which often excludes openly queer and trans men and boys. My positioning as a queer cisgender female who cares very much about and works as a mentor of several young men and boys of color requires this discourse.

The young man I have mentored the longest is now a college graduate and currently works as a teacher in Washington, DC. He is biracial and identifies as gay though he insists that sexuality is fluid and does not believe that he should have to identify. The next protégé is a senior at a Washington, DC, university. He is Black, and he identifies as gay. The third protégé is currently taking courses at a local community college. He is Black, and he identifies as bisexual. The fourth protégé is now a freshman in college. He is Latino, and he identifies as gay. I list them in this order because there is a progression in my mentoring practice as a result of my experiences with each of them. None of them openly identified as gay in high school, and the majority had mastered the art of "covering" until they were out of high school. Yoshino (2007) describes "covering" as "toning down" aspects of our identity that don't resonate with the mainstream. As I mentioned earlier, our organization was set up to serve young people of color and, as a result, our mentoring framework has always been a critical one. I recognize that the young people I am mentoring require a mentoring relationship that mirrors their home culture, does not see them as deficient, and helps them to navigate a world that is often hostile and oppositional to who they are. With this understanding, I strive to help all of my protégés become more aware of themselves in relationship to institutions, especially educational ones, as I aid them in searching for the college that best serves their needs and desires, completing college applications, applying for financial aid, and making the connections they need to continue being successful outside of the program.

It was in working with these young men that I began to understand how their age, sexuality, and race intersected to create a myriad of challenges in their coming-of-age process. And I also wish to note that the youngest of my protégés benefited greatly from the mentoring relationships I had previously engaged in with others. I make this point to highlight the idea that mentors are also beneficiaries of the mentoring relationship; it is a sort of mutual exchange, with the protégé teaching the mentor as much as he or she is learning. Consider the fact that each of these young men was navigating a dynamic unlike many of their peers and at a formative time in their lives. Their very existence as young, raced, and queer men required that I find ways to navigate each of these aspects of their identities to help them survive and thrive.

Again, we must look at foundational research to guide our efforts. Intersectionality is an important component of critical race theory and necessary to consider when dealing with LGBTQQ youth. It should not be used exclusively in the analysis of this population but is crucial to including them in conversations so often centered on race and class. Intersectionality deals with examining critically the ways that different aspects of marginalized identities converge to create multiple axes of disadvantage and oppression. Delgado and Stefancic (2012) define *intersectionality* as "the examination of race, sex, class, national origin, and sexual orientation, and how their combination plays out in various settings" (p. 57). Kimberle Crenshaw coined the term in 1989 in her seminal critique of feminist theory. In it, she utilizes the metaphor of an intersection to describe the multiple and sometimes simultaneous ways in which Black women are impacted by "blind" legal policies (Crenshaw, 1989). This groundbreaking concept is necessary to critical mentoring work because it helps mentoring and youth development professionals to understand that the young people with whom we are working may not fit neatly into one identity designation. They may, in fact, be young, queer, of color, and gender nonconforming. These identifiers are not neatly divorced from one another, not for the youth who identify and not for the society that perceives them as such. Dealing with youth as solely Afro-Latino, or solely poor, or solely queer without considering how each of these identities intersects and overlaps to hinder a mentoring relationship is dubious. Conjointly, ignoring the ways that our young protégés are impacted as a result of societal biases against each or all of these identities gets in the way of doing critical mentoring work that aims to look more closely at how mentoring can address how they are marginalized.

So, in each of these areas—age, race, and sexuality—getting to the heart of how they impacted my protégés and how I could help them was of primary importance. Furthermore, my limited understanding of language and issues, even as a member of the LGBTQQ community, meant that I needed to move beyond metanarratives or common understandings of these matters to be able to ascertain them fully.

Age, Race, and Sexuality

Intersectionality helped me to understand that each of my protégés was not only navigating sexuality but also dealing with different identifiers that compounded to make their lives much more complicated. They were experiencing challenges as youth, as racialized beings in a White world, and as queer men. That my protégés were in high school when our mentoring relationship formed meant that they were at a critical juncture in their development and battling issues that come with being young. As adults, we often minimize the complexity of teenage thought; we question their judgment and ability to make sound decisions, and while I am not saying that young people are perfect, their ability to process and understand the complexity of the world is often very acute. However, few of us stop to talk with and listen to them, so we end up judging them based on preconceived notions of what youth culture is, and we often sum that up as being somewhat reckless, immature, and driven by sexual desires. One could argue that these characteristics fit many adults as well, so those representations cannot adequately summarize the maturity levels of all young people. However, this attitude, that teenagers know very little and that they need to grow up, so to speak, prohibits many adults from understanding that teens do, in fact, have very real and honest understandings of identity.

As a result of this ageism, teens experience a lack of freedom to express identity openly and to use voice because their perceived "place" in the world is often a subordinate one. Some of their confusion has less to do with their lack of maturity than it does with having to navigate the ideals and expectations of adults around them who have established notions of gender roles, sexuality, and so on. So, they have to come to a sort of consensus about how they feel and who they are while also dealing with established societal rules and mores, guided primarily by adults. It is critical that mentors and youth development professionals working with LGBTQQ youth recognize that as "children" societal norms have positioned young people in a way that does not allow them to express themselves, which has ramifications for identity expression.

Then there is a certain lack of freedom, often taken for granted by adults, to explore their sexuality. Most teens are living with parents or other adult authority figures, so they have limited room to act on their feelings. I remember sharing with my mentor, and this was when I was in college, that I might be a lesbian. Her response was shocking: She recommended that I engage in a mutual sexual encounter with another woman to see how I felt about the experience. I wish to be clear that I am not advocating "promiscuity" among teens. Instead, I am noting that in the adult world we can make decisions about how we engage sexually and for teenagers this exploration simply isn't an option. Living with parents under the rules of most parents, teens cannot openly experiment. This is not to say that they lack experiences; we know that many of them are still exploring, but that exploration is happening in a less healthy, more rushed, and public way.

Peers also pose a problem, in that bullying and peer pressure are still very real aspects of their lives. All of my protégés shared that one of their primary concerns in being open about their identities in high school was that they were firsthand witnesses of blatant homoantagonism on their schools' campuses and that most of these acts were unaddressed by adults in these spaces. Teenagers are therefore forming supposed identities based on societal expectations, parental expectations, and lack of freedom to express and explore—all of this in a hypersexualized society and with few opportunities to connect with caring adult mentors and programs that have nuanced understandings of who they are.

Then we have the issue of sexuality, which you can already easily identify as intersecting with age. So, the biggest problem here is teenagers' ability to identify, to name, and to own their sexuality. Navigating a heteronormative and patriarchal society in which homoantagonism continues to be pervasive, LGBTQQ youth must be very careful about how they express who they are. In fact, when speaking to the oldest of my protégés, he would often remind me, "No one ever begins a conversation about sexuality with heterosexuals using the question 'So when did you know you were straight?'" The idea that heterosexuality is "normal" and homosexuality is "abnormal," "experimental," or "a phase" creates a sense of trepidation about identifying. Each of my protégés knew he was homosexual but was afraid to identify for various reasons including a very real concern for his physical and emotional well-being. One of them noted, "There were very specific incidents that would happen in class, when other students would make particular comments about me, about my sexuality. You were supposed to be this big masculine figure, and I felt as if I was basically trying to hide that side of me."

The issue of sexuality therefore comes with typical challenges. LGBTQQ issues have been more openly discussed in the last decade, but not in the manner that allows for the progressive ways our young people express identities. Savin-Williams (2005) describes this generational difference in his book *The New Gay Teenager*. He explains that contemporary youth are "increasingly redefining, reinterpreting, and renegotiating their sexuality such that possessing a gay, lesbian, or bisexual identity is practically meaningless" (p. 36). Intersectionality becomes even more indispensable for "new" youth as mentors work to address identities that are in constant negotiation, both by those who possess them and by the society that judges them. This fluid expression—youth that don't acknowledge or purposely defy gender binaries—can create whole other levels of apprehension for many adults. Identifying, naming, and owning sexuality as well as an inability to express openly for fear of societal isolation and discrimination are points that mentoring and youth development professionals must address in mentoring relationships.

But race still comes to bear in this conversation. An important issue that arose when working with my protégés was identifying "gayness as Whiteness." In each descriptor of their journey, they made statements about not wanting to be a cliché or a stereotype, and when asked to unpack that, they mostly described the effeminate White male so often portrayed in the media. Their statements were profound. In fact, many folks of color in the LGBTQQ community have argued that our most visible fight, the fight for marriage equality, centered Whiteness as often as possible. We worked so hard to align ourselves with dominant ideals of White and heteronormative society in an attempt to appear as much like dominant society as possible in order to earn marriage equality. This means that much of what these young men and a generation of queer youth of color were watching in the form of documentaries, news coverage, and paper ads, systematically excluded them, excluded gays of color, queer women, and the transgendered. Even contemporary film privileges the gay, White, and male narrative, centering the gay civil rights struggle on stories like those portrayed in *Milk* and *Brokeback Mountain* (Kohnen, 2015). Most recently, *Stonewall,* which hit theaters amid resounding clashes about its lack of verisimilitude in relationship to the known history of transgender and queers of color involvement in the defining moment, carries this exclusion forward. Melanie Kohnen's (2015) work in this area details this process of excluding queers of color, particularly in cardinal LGBTQQ civil rights moments, especially those portrayed in film. The result of this exclusion means that even spaces in which queer youth of color thought they might be more welcome did not reflect the richness of their identity. It means that the LGBTQQ community operated in binaries similar to those of the heterosexual community. And, though LGBTQQ folks of color exist, it was hard for my protégés to visualize themselves as members of this community.

The concept of "gayness as Whiteness" is problematic. If our young queers of color see images of their sexuality only as centric to Whiteness, as othered dually, in regard to race and sexuality, they cannot understand themselves. These young men had not problematized their homosexuality as much as they had problematized its lack of identification with their racialized experiences. They wanted much more to be Black or Latino than they did to be gay and were forced into that binary by an LGBTQQ community who told them that they did not exist. The oldest protégé noted, "It took for me to go to college to really appreciate and see diversity. I got to see that diversity in a positive way so that it made me feel more comfortable and be more comfortable with myself." Another protégé said, "You are just trying to make everyone else see that you are this strong Black man, you are just trying to be a role model, an example for the Black community at the school, and if you are labeled gay, then that just takes so much from it."

As a mentor whose purpose was to provide guidance, providing critical mentorship was challenging when it came to the intersection of age, sexuality, and race. It is for that reason that I include this chapter. I had thought through mentoring young people who were racialized, I had thought through mentoring young people who were of low socioeconomic status, I had thought through mentoring LGBTQQ youth, but I had not considered how these things might come together to create the need for another level of support. Working with these young men helped me realize that LGBTQQ youth are often left out of many of these discussions and LGBTQQ youth of color even more so.

Mentoring them left me with more questions than answers about how to help each of them navigate all of these very complex issues. How would I remain sensitive to their need to "cover" though I knew they were struggling to name and own their identities? In fact, I did directly ask one of my protégés whether he was gay. He denied his sexual identity and later described himself as being offended by my asking. How would I respect the nature of our relationship and also abide by the requirements of their parents? Should I make explicit connections between them and James Baldwin, Richard Rodriguez, Audre Lorde? How I navigated issues of youth, race, and sexuality with each of my protégés varied from the first protégé to those I am currently working with. While I maintain ongoing relationships with each of them, the lessons they taught me benefit the queer youth I mentor currently. I was more sensitive and open with the last protégé discussed in this chapter, having watched the results I had with the others. As a result, he enjoyed receiving writings by Baldwin, Rodriguez, and Lorde, and we spoke explicitly about the issues he had and would likely confront as he came of age.

Think Differently

Much of what I have described has been challenging for other mentors and youth development professionals as well. One of the many reasons critical mentoring was developed was to begin opening up the mentoring field to language and praxis that would address the needs of protégés like the ones I describe. In working with LGBTQQ youth and young people who are marginalized and minoritized in other ways, it is essential to think differently. Our young people have progressed in a manner that few of us can imagine, and though they are fully capable, they require guidance and support in new and innovative ways. We also must consider that young people do not necessarily share the same ideas about critical issues that we do. I had a hard time grasping the concept of gender nonconforming until a protégé taught me that I challenge gender binaries daily in the ways that I dress. They insisted that I see myself more clearly to help me understand them. And this work is necessary. I've navigated mentoring and youth development spaces that are focused on men and boys of color and the discussions are typically centered on race or class with no acknowledgment of sexuality, and very little to no discussion of gender norms. Intersectional conversations are necessary! Young Black men and boys can also be queer, trans, or gender nonconforming. Even as groups that serve young men and boys of color concentrate so diligently on the harm to Black and Brown bodies, they fail to acknowledge how social mores and norms resist, disrupt, traumatize, and enact violence upon the discursive fluidity of bodies. So trans bodies are othered, don't fit neatly into the gendered imagination, and therefore aren't worthy of mentoring support or protection of any form. Then trans bodies of color are othered in more than one way, finding little acceptance in wider society, little acceptance in the LGBTQQ community, and little acceptance in communities of color.

I have been guilty of inadvertently silencing LGBTQQ youth as well. During National Mentoring Month, my organization puts on a series of critical mentoring events to highlight the importance of mentoring from this perspective. In 2016, we held a panel discussion on the mentoring experiences of Black men and boys. We invited protégés to make up the panel so that we could hear directly from young people. It wasn't until the end of the discussion that I greeted one of the protégés

I discussed earlier in this chapter. He had been sitting in the audience listening. It suddenly struck me that we had not included queer or trans men in the panel discussion. We had been so focused on discussing race that we neglected to include Black queers. Even with a keen focus on critical issues, one can miss the mark.

I have been using the terms *reimagine* and *rethink* to help the mentoring and youth development fields advance in their thinking. These words remain apropos. It is not enough to move forward without critiquing and recreating. Bettina Love (in press) offers mentors a particular way to rethink mentoring in her article "'She Has a Real Connection with Them': Reimagining and Expanding Our Definitions of Black Masculinity and Mentoring in Education Through Female Masculinity." As the title suggests, Love questions whether Black men are the only ones who can effectively mentor Black men and boys. She expresses her desire to push the envelope, asking us to look beyond "traditional norms of sex and gender identities/performances" (Love, in press, p. 1). She cites an example of a Black female who identifies as lesbian who is a competent mentor of the Black boys she engages. These mentoring relationships are situated within the context of schools with specific implications for that work, but the crux of the article challenges notions of gender identities, the concept of masculinity and sexuality. Much of what Love suggests here will likely make some uncomfortable and challenge our rooted ideas around these issues, but engaging as a critical mentor is about being able to reimagine relationships and spaces. We must also consider that many of our antiquated ideas about gender are no longer useful to the young people we are serving and forcing them to operate in ways that are comfortable for us is not the answer. Working with youth at intersections may make some of us uncomfortable, but we have choices about the work we engage in. In my job as a mentor trainer I have been very clear about my charge to mentors: Do no harm. If working with a particular type of youth does not suit you, then respectfully request to be matched with another youth. Let the program decide where to utilize you best, but do not engage in harmful practices that can traumatize a young person and negatively alter his or her trajectory. Young people working with mentors are looking for support systems and advocates, not an extension of the marginalization they find so easily in society.

Mentoring and youth development practitioners have a significant amount of work to do when addressing the needs of LGBTQQ youth and LGBTQQ youth of color. With so many issues confronting this population the need to approach the relationship in critical ways is a good place to begin. If we don't begin to interrogate our work around this group of youth, much of the work we are doing in other spaces that we deem critical or revolutionary will have been lost.

Questions to Ask

- How do we train mentors to work better with LGBTQQ youth?
- Are we having intersectional conversations with and about the young people we serve? Or plan to serve?
- How do we ensure that we include the voices of our LGBTQQ youth and respect their privacy and identifying processes?
- Are we challenging our notions of gender and sexuality as we work to support young people in their processes?
- Have we worked to include the LGBTQQ community in the work we do?
- Do we have structures in place to ensure that LGBTQQ youth are not in contact with volunteers or staff who may not be comfortable with their identities?
- How do we better understand the concept of intersectionality?
- How does intersectionality have an impact on the young people with whom we work and the communities in which we work?

Actions to Take

- *Be intersectional.* When setting up programs to serve youth of color, don't assume you won't have youth at intersections. Our society is a truly diverse one. Programs created to serve Latinos may also have to deal with Afro-Latinos and confront the complexity of those dual identities. Similarly, programs set up to help Black men and boys may also have to deal with transgender men and boys and confront the complexity of those dual identities. Learn to think in intersectional ways when approaching the mentoring process. When identifying issues that arise with race, stop to consider how gender might also play a role. When dealing with a conflict or challenge around gender, stop to look at how class might also play a role. Be cognizant of the varied ways that identities are stratified in your life and reflect on how different aspects of you are marginalized or privileged. When you can see how identities and how society perceives them operate in your own life, it will help you to see them at work in the lives of the young people you serve. There are activities you can use to map out your different identities and then highlight which identities are privileged and which are marginalized. Such activities are a starting point for reflection and discussion. This also means engaging in discourse in board meetings, staff meetings, or community workshops to process through these difficult points. Mentoring and youth development programs need to develop processes for continual reflection that encourage nuanced understanding of identities and the ways that society views them. To do so means engaging in critical training with facilitators who can help the board and staff understand the language and theories related to the concept as well as identify realistic ways this all plays out in the community being served. In addition, it should not be assumed that marginalization and minoritization exist simply and neatly on one axis. Understand and help youth navigate the myriad ways their identifiers can have an impact on them and work with them to name, challenge, and change those impacts.

- *Challenge metanarratives.* It is of particular importance when working with LGBTQQ youth to challenge the narrative that "gayness is Whiteness." Help young people to understand that there is a history of diversity within the LGBTQQ community as well as contemporary examples. The notion of living history, pointing out contemporary figures that look like them, is critical. Embark upon an ongoing history project, both within the organization and with mentors and protégés. Learn about local figures first, highlighting diverse figures from the community, then branch out. Highlight figures that are "lesser" known particularly because of their identities. Find every opportunity to center those histories and to highlight the many contributions that these people have made. For example, when talking about Dr. Martin Luther King Jr. as we do nationally every year, emphasize the contribution of the queer activist and organizer Bayard Rustin, who played such a pivotal role in the Black civil rights movement. Examine why he is underrecognized, making explicit connections to his identity and the need to ensure the movement had broad appeal. Exploring a figure like Rustin, who worked so ardently on behalf of Blacks, can help young people challenge the idea that they are less raced because of their sexual or gender identity.

- *Recruit diversely.* Just because your particular mentoring or youth development program is not centered on LGBTQQ issues doesn't mean you can't engage the community. Recruit volunteers, staff, and mentors diversely, inviting members of the LGBTQQ community to play an active role. When race is discussed we often make the argument that including people of color is not just a good idea for youth of color, but a good idea for White youth too. The same can be said for sexuality and gender. Recruiting members of the LGBTQQ community is not just good for queer youth; it's good for heterosexual and cisgender youth as well. Our young people need to see models of adults from a range of experiences and identities. Make a real and concerted effort to include a diverse range of identities on your board, on your staff, and among your volunteers and mentors. Do this explicitly. Your organization should reflect the diversity that exists in the community. If you have to look in unlikely places to find them, do so. Our young people are worth it.

- *Be trained.* If you are unsure about how to approach the needs of LGBTQQ youth and LGBTQQ youth of color, get some training. A wealth of information is available from local and national organizations that do this work. Often, college campuses house centers that can help you find the local training and resources you need to serve these youth, such as the Queer

Resource Center of Pomona College in California or an LGBT resource center.

To do critical mentoring work, we must be engaged at different levels; a real critical consciousness means looking beyond our small corners and doing work that is holistic, global, and in recognition of our interconnectedness. One specific call to action is for the work of My Brother's Keeper to confront silence around LGBTQQ issues, to include the LGBTQQ youth community in the work, and to learn and hear from these young people, as well as to help young LGBTQQ men to build a future. Also, we must rethink structures that center antiquated ideas around masculinity and find out how queer and trans men have always impacted movements like My Brother's Keeper.

Critical mentoring means having the fortitude and tools to tackle complicated issues such as sexuality, gender, and how they intersect. Mentoring and youth development professionals must leverage critical frameworks to better understand young people and to help them. When mentoring and youth development professionals are undergoing training they need to hear about ethical issues, the purpose of mentoring, effective elements of mentoring, and also how to leverage that human connection to help youth see themselves in relationship to discriminatory structures. We have to find folks who are willing to do this kind of work, and we have to link them to thriving mentoring communities.

5

COLLECTING COMMUNITY-CENTERED AND CULTURALLY RELEVANT DATA

The business operations or data person in any mentoring or youth development organization has been waiting for this chapter. These individuals may have enjoyed reading and thinking about the ideas in this book and believe they are great. They would love to ensure that their organization is on board, but they are worried about what this kind of work means for the board of directors, funders, and resourced stakeholders. They are looking for data, how to do this critical work and still shape a fundable nonprofit narrative. These are reasonable concerns. We won't be able to do this work without the funding required to sustain us. And, if those of us who are conscious of and interested in doing critical mentoring don't find ways of making this work fundable, other organizations who are less critical surely will. Shawn Dove, CEO of the Campaign for Black Male Achievement, said it best: "This is a love movement, and there is no logic model for love" (Dove, 2015). It is true that critical mentoring is about love, and although there may be no way to include love in a logic model, there are some pretty rigorous and tangible ways to collect data that illustrate what we can do with critical mentoring.

Appreciative Inquiry

Appreciative inquiry (AI) is a plausible beginning for organizations that employ critical mentoring. Most notable because it abandons "deficit-oriented approaches," AI has been used in the academic and business worlds alike (Cooperrider, Whitney, & Stavros, 2008). True to its name, AI is about identifying strengths or what works well with people, systems, and organizations (Cooperrider et al., 2008). Cooperrider and colleagues (2008) note, "AI is based on the simple assumption that every organization has something that works well, and those strengths can be the starting point for creating positive change" (p. 3). Developed by David Cooperrider in 1980, AI has been used as a base time and again to transform communities, schools, and organizations. There are several important elements to note about AI, but understanding that it is built on something called a "Constructionist Principle" is fundamental. The Constructionist Principle says that "social knowledge and organizational destiny are interwoven" (Cooperrider et al., 2008, p. 10), that from the very beginning approach and questions asked are the foundational elements of the institutional fabric. Liberating the mentoring and youth development world from deficit-based approaches has been discussed at length in this book. AI works for mentoring and youth development work in two paramount ways: it helps the organization doing the work to focus specifically on what it is already doing well and to strengthen it, and it makes the organization responsible for identifying the strengths of the people and communities with whom it is working. Rather than moving into communities to fix what might be considered as wrong with them, organizations focus on finding what is right within communities and alter their strategies and programming to build on what's right. Consider the possibilities here: nonprofits wanting to highlight and build upon what communities are already doing well and partnering with communities to provide additional resources that support that work, resulting in greater impact and widened capacity for all. Much of this text has examined ways to change the organizational trajectories of those doing mentoring and youth development work, and although we have considered deficit-oriented approaches in one-to-one relationships, we have not considered deficit-oriented approaches when it comes to a holistic way of thinking as an organization. Much of what nonprofit ventures do is highlight a problem or need that requires services to be addressed. While highlighting need is necessary to state a case for services, if it includes all of what the community isn't but must be, then nonprofits miss the mark and move in the direction of problematizing the youth and communities they serve from the outset.

AI changes a needs statement from one of disapproval and problem finding to one of appreciation and valuing. Mentoring and youth development organizations should be looking to enhance, not displace and replace. AI addresses the needs statement in their paradigm for organizational change. In the problem-solving model, which is the way most mentor and youth development organizations currently operate, they list "felt need" or "identification of problem" as the first step (Cooperrider et al., 2008). In the AI model, which is what mentoring and youth development organizations should be using, they identify "appreciating" or "valuing the best of what is" as the first step (Cooperrider et al., 2008). These are not just shifts in diction; these are changes in approach and make all the difference when doing work with folks who have been pervasively demonized and problematized. If the basis of service is fixing, not partnering to enhance, then organizations have missed the mark as well as the opportunity to do critical work. Additionally, the grassroots work already being done in these communities should serve as a conduit for AI. Tapping into what these grassroots organizations do best and then helping to give them the resources to take that programming to a higher level is preferable. Doing this does not require shifting the role of the mentoring or youth development organization to "funder." Again, we must reimagine ways to engage with one another. If a grassroots nonprofit in an urban city is doing incredible and culturally relevant mentoring work with young women and girls of color and there is a major nonprofit in the same city engaging in the same work, why shouldn't the two look at what the other has to offer? Each should be looking at ways to partner and collaborate on scaling up impact, widening the resource pool, and exchanging valuable knowledge. The nonprofit sector knows well the funding imperative of partner networks and scale; many funders are moving in the direction of supporting collaboratives that can show more extensive work and more impact for their dollar. Grassroots organizations may not have as many financial resources available to them, but they may have the most diverse pool of volunteer mentors available. Major nonprofits may not have culturally relevant programming, but they may have the funding capacity to support the implementation of such a system and will most certainly need help from grassroots organizations to do so.

Furthermore, mentoring and youth development organizations desiring to do critical mentoring work need to recognize that many of the communities deemed "serviceable" often have a host of underrecognized and underappreciated resources that can be built into thriving systems for young people. Elders in the community who may not be formally connected to programs might be experienced in business entrepreneurship and ownership, something that youth find very valuable. However, no one asks the elders to volunteer as mentors or provide workshops or offer program support in this arena because the community itself is deemed an economic failure. This missed opportunity is one that could connect the young people we serve to what works well in their communities, support the forging of intergenerational connections, and place value on knowledge indigenous to the communities.

AI asks us to identify what works well in communities. It asks us to identify the wealth of the community, what they bring to the table, and to work to achieve next levels. While AI provides us with foundational processes to inform our work, narrative research moves us into the realm of getting more nuanced data out of the critical work we are doing in order to shape a narrative that illustrates the complexity of critical mentoring and tells the nonprofit story in ways funders can understand.

Narrative Research

Shaping a narrative that stakeholders and funders can support is essential to a successful nonprofit organization. For mentoring and youth development organizations this narrative is even more valuable because we work with young people who require a concentrated set of services. Many of us already use data to illustrate what we do well. Ensuring that our data are not only quantitative but also have a rigorous qualitative approach is important. Storytelling, especially in the context of mentoring and youth development organizations, can be perceived as explicitly manipulative, which is something to carefully take into consideration. However, telling stories that often go untold in ways outside of the norm and on platforms that are not typically provided may be of more value than recognized.

Narrative research is described as having three forms. The first form is centered on "recounting past events" directly from those who have experienced them. The second form seeks to "explore stories" that range in length, type, and form and includes stories that are not directly experienced by the storyteller (Andrews, Squire, & Tamboukou, 2008). This form also includes various types of storytelling in media. Because it can also include visual media, I include the concept of photovoice within this form. Photovoice is a process whereby participants share their stories via photography (C. Wang & Burris, 1997). It is especially compelling in concert with narratives because the two together provide a fuller exploration of youth and community context, providing rich data for mentoring and youth development organizations doing critical work. The third form of narrative research is narratives that are coconstructed or jointly built during an interview process, informal conversation, or other types of exchange between people (Andrews et al., 2008). It should be noted that narrative research is not simple; it's a complex and evolving way of capturing, analyzing, and sharing data. Narrative research requires time to collect and make sense of data but is worth careful consideration when doing critical mentoring work because of its emphasis on the living, human, and evolving nature of narrative. The humanity in narrative research is why it should be fully utilized in nonprofit work.

As mentioned earlier, many of the communities we deem serviceable are problematized and dehumanized. Narrative or storytelling is a platform for voice, dynamic expression, and illustration of humanity, something ignored in many marginalized and minoritized communities, sometimes even by the nonprofits who claim to be serving them. Again, consider the problem or needs statement, which often utilizes faceless statistics to demonstrate that these communities have failed in some way and now require services to right their wrongs. The richness of narrative data is endless, giving organizations ample content to inform the work they are doing and share the work they have already done.

Utilizing both structured and unstructured processes, staff working for the Youth Mentoring Action Network sit down with protégés on a regular basis to engage in narrative research processes. In fact, collecting narrative data is a regular part of what we do. We engage in storytelling as a communicative process with protégés and transition from using narrative as a mode of communication to a mode of data collecting. We have established a narrative data collection plan that begins with interviews, focus groups, and photovoice projects; utilizes interviews and focus groups regularly during the program year; and then culminates in exit interviews that gather final thoughts and reflections. While there are established sets of questions for staff to work with, we encourage them to be responsive to participants, feeling free to ask additional questions or alter questions as they see fit. The data collected are analyzed in reliable ways and are shared only with explicit permission from protégés, or their parents if they are underage. We also collect quantitative data to keep track of how often mentors and protégés meet, how many program activities each of them engages in, how many set goals were reached, high school graduation rates, and college acceptance rates. We are acutely aware that qualitative research often requires more rigor and time, so we collect long-term data, first yearlong data and then from year to year until our protégés graduate from high school. Having a more nuanced story to tell, outside of percentages, accomplishes several goals. First, we can connect to the young people we serve. From the very beginning, they understand that we are listening to them and centering them, valuing their stories and utilizing those stories to inform our work. Second, the relationships between mentor and protégé are typically stronger and more resilient because of a sense of connectedness between them. Third, and finally, we always have ample data to share with stakeholders regarding the nuances of the work we do.

Chris is a protégé in the Youth Mentoring Action Network program. He has been working with the same two mentors for four years now, since his freshman year of high school. Chris is an Afro-Latino male who performs well academically, is engaged in several school activities, and appears as a typically well-adjusted youth. Through our narrative collecting process, staff and mentors in our program learned a lot more about Chris and his context than we would have without it. When Chris joined us a freshman, his interview stories revealed a great deal about his relationship with his mother: how close they were, how much wisdom he believed she offered him, the power to express himself, and much more. It was also clear, however, that his mom had been sick. As a sophomore in high school, Chris lost his mother. Knowing well how close and connected he felt to her and understanding that his need to express his loss, be supported, and be encouraged would be great, we doubled our efforts to support him and included him in our programming in various ways. Soon after he lost his mother, Chris moved to live with his adult sister, her husband, and her son, another challenging adjustment for Chris, who was still reeling from his mother's death. Again, much of this story was uncovered utilizing narrative research processes. Chris maintained an excellent school record and stayed involved in school activities and in the mentoring program, but he struggled to adjust to his new reality. His mentors were actively engaged in providing him additional support and worked with his family to be sure Chris was well looked after. In Chris's senior year, he applied for a Posse Scholarship, a scholarship awarded in partnership with a community organization to give underrepresented youth the opportunity to attend a university for free. Chris was awarded the scholarship and placed at Brunel University in Pennsylvania. However, the award and other coming-of-age events like the prom and graduation were marred by Chris's loss. Once again Chris's mentors gave him the support he needed, helping him to find a summer job, encouraging him to find healthy ways to grieve, and ensuring he stayed on top of his course work.

Chris's "story" is particularly important to my point about doing critical work because it illustrates how much we can learn about the youth with whom we work. Sometimes we are serving so many young people that we are unaware of the impact we are having. Nonprofits often depend on mentors to share stories about the young people they are mentoring with staff. Typically, this informal storytelling isn't informed by evidence-based processes that provide the mentors with usable tools. Additionally, what we learned about Chris was not limited to knowing about this sequence of events in his life; it was much more about what kind of protégé we were working with and what we could learn to improve our ability to help him. The by-product was having a powerful story to tell stakeholders. In connection with AI, we learned how important Chris's bond with his mother was and how much family support he had. We learned how resilient Chris was, how he was able to grieve in healthy ways and still move forward to accomplish his goals. We learned that healthy and loving connections were important to Chris and that he expected his mentor to provide that for him. As a nonprofit organization focused on helping young people get through high school and into college, we feel that Chris's is one of our most inspiring stories, a testament that the guidance and support of a mentor helped him to navigate some of life's most difficult circumstances.

What if the Youth Mentoring Action Network hadn't grasped the concept of narrative research to begin with? What if, instead, we focused only on quantitative metrics to ascertain whether we were doing our jobs? Would we have known or paid attention to Chris's story as an example of the more nuanced mentoring work that we do? It's hard to say exactly, but I am sure that our youth-centered philosophy, which makes us more apt to engage in qualitative research, helps us to shape a powerful narrative about mentoring and about the critical mentoring work that we do. By our quantitative data, Chris was doing well academically and thus needed very little support. He was getting through high school, he was college bound, we were providing him with as many resources in those areas as we could, but we would have missed another level of support, an opportunity to double our efforts and share an incredible story of resilience with our stakeholders and funders. We also would have assumed, given that our immediate goals were academic support and college access, that Chris wasn't in need of help or didn't meet the requirements for support. Don't think of narrative research as a way to "toot your horn"; instead, use it as a tool to get more complex and nuanced data, which we must do if we are to share critical work with stakeholders. If not for narrative research, how do we share the knowledge, expertise, or critical networks already at work in these communities and with a deeper understanding of how to serve?

Mentoring and youth development organizations have to move beyond metrics. Critical mentoring requires that we examine the ways that multiple and often adverse elements come together to marginalize and minoritize our young people. Although data give us some of that information, they do not help us to understand the myriad ways that this happens, nor do they include what is needed to be able to attach a human narrative to those data. Stories are rich and powerful, and if captured and recounted well and accurately, they can illustrate the challenges, triumphs, pains, and joys of youth who exist in contexts that are toxic. In fact, narrative research has helped these very groups to reclaim power in spaces where their voices are not valued and where their bodies and lives are often minimized by data sets.

Utilizing narratives helps organizations better understand who they are serving and provides rich data that can be used to share with stakeholders and funders. If mentoring and youth development nonprofits want funders to understand the imperative of critical mentoring work, then we must move beyond traditional nonprofit trajectories.

Empowerment Evaluation

After mentoring and youth development organizations have established their initial approach and implemented ways to capture and analyze quantitative and qualitative data, they must undergo an evaluation process. Evaluations are used as a checks-and-balances system to ensure that organizations are doing the work they say they are. Typically these evaluations are steeped in anxiety because organizations must look for neutral evaluators outside their programs to scrutinize their processes and provide a detailed report to them as well as their stakeholders. Every organization, whether a K–12 school, a for-profit corporation, or a nonprofit organization, has and should have evaluative processes in place because they are a valuable way to ensure ongoing and systematic growth and repair. Like the other forms of data collection and analysis platforms I've presented in this chapter, the need to utilize a process outside of typical scope is necessary. Every element of how we go about our work matters. We can't implement one process in the hopes of doing culturally relevant work and then undermine it with another process that doesn't value the first.

Empowerment evaluation, a powerful tool for community work, is a culturally relevant way to do evaluation because it includes the community, makes data pertinent, and makes data usable. It was developed by Stanford professor David Fetterman in 1994 and has been used in various contexts all over the world to help "communities plan, implement, assess and improve their work" (Fetterman & Wandersman, 2015, p. 29). Following 10 essential principles, this evaluation process is about guiding community work in ways that are both credible and actionable. The 10 principles are improvement, community ownership, inclusion, democratic participation, social justice, community knowledge, evidence-based strategies, capacity building, organizational learning, and accountability (Fetterman, Kaftarian, & Wandersman, 2015).

There are several approaches for empowerment evaluation, but I choose to highlight the three-step approach because of its simplicity and ease of use. The three steps are working on a mission, "taking stock" of current practices, and planning for the future (Fetterman et al., 2015, p. 53). Each step is about utilizing the 10 aforementioned principles to inform the process, ensuring that there is group ownership and consensus. For the mission aspect, a group of stakeholders gather to look at the mission of the organization to consider whether it reflects their "shared vision." For the first step, stakeholders are instructed to "generate statements that reflect their mission" (p. 55) and then these are posted for the group to consider and reflect upon. The process is collaborative and provokes discussion about what their shared goals are. The second step involves "taking stock" of activities. This process includes having the stakeholders look closely at the activities that the organization engages in and how that is a reflection of their mission. In other words, do the activities align with the mission? They are also asked to rate those activities in order of how important they are to the mission or the organization's goals. Finally, participants are asked to look at their findings and utilize them in a plan for their future. Here they "generate goals, strategies and credible evidence" (p. 55) to ensure that they have something to follow and remain on track.

What undergirds empowerment evaluation is what makes it such a powerful practice: It puts the process of evaluation, before having been relegated to an outside observer, in the hands of the community doing the work; it builds an organizational culture of data and evidence collection that is collaborative; and it ensures the results are immediately usable for the organization and its stakeholders. These processes are essential for mentoring and youth development organizations doing critical mentoring work. Again, it's about reimagining spaces, how data are perceived and how they are used to grow the work. We may intuitively know what the work is accomplishing, but how do we put that into credible forms that undergird our organizational structures and that are included in our reports to stakeholders? Empowerment evaluation works regarding its processes but will not be the process it is meant to be if the term *community* is not properly defined here. This book has highlighted time and again the idea that community should be those who are being served. Explicitly stated, if your mentoring or youth development organization is located in the "hood," a colloquialism for the neighborhood but most often associated with urban regions, folks from the "hood" should be included in the evaluation process, just as they should be volunteers, staff, and board members.

Critical mentoring requires that because the young people being served are vital aspects of the organization they be engaged as coevaluators, going through this process alongside the board members, CEOs, and staff. Who better to inform our progress and process than those who are supposed to benefit? Empowerment evaluation is a research-based process for doing just that. It includes parents, protégés, and community members alongside those inside the organization to evaluate progress and plan for future work. It is unlike other processes in that it centers the community and focuses on providing tools and resources that aid them as they go about working in their communities. It is a good tool for any organization, but particularly important for those following the path of critical mentoring because it provides us with a credible platform to engage the youth and the communities we serve.

This chapter is not intended to be a means of simplifying the ways we collect data; rather, it is meant to widen the discussion of what constitutes data and highlight processes that help us to be culturally relevant in our research and evaluation of mentoring and youth development programs. To be sure, we exist in a high-stakes and competitive funding market that often values quantitative data. And, quantitative data are necessary, but used solely they leave out valuable information and often nuanced information that highlights the positives of the communities in which we operate. Data collected from qualitative and quantitative processes are both considered evidence based but are viewed differently by different audiences and for different purposes. While federal grant funds may require quantitative data collected by researchers and evaluators, it is important that our internal processes allow us to collect data in as many ways as possible so that we learn to value what isn't often valued in other, more formal realms. This chapter also highlights the importance of having a data collection and analysis strategy that utilizes various approaches and highlights as much nuanced information as possible utilizing both quantitative and qualitative processes. Hiring a researcher and evaluator versed in mixed-methods approaches and approaches that function as ways to value marginalized communities is as important as hiring a statistician for research and evaluation of your programming. Finally, many of the national organizations I've mentioned in this book are respective examples of AI or PAR projects at work. The Black Youth Project, for example, embodies both processes as youth are centered and directly involved in the research and analysis of the problems facing them and their communities, while they also place emphasis on valuing and building on what works well. Cathy Cohen (2009), a scholar, is an ardent advocate for this collaborative process.

It is important to note again that power sharing is crucial for critical mentoring work. All of these research-based suggestions are made so that practitioners understand that there are alternative ways to do nonprofit business and that those ways do not have to be steeped in antiquated ideas about how service is done. And, most important, these processes do not have to be done "to" the youth and "to" the communities we work in, nor do they have to be about devaluing what our young people bring to the table to highlight or increase our own value. They must be done with our youth and communities if we are to be critical and useful to them.

Questions to Ask

- What are our current processes for collecting data, if any?
- Are those current processes inclusive of our youth and the communities they live in?
- How can we alter our current data collection and analysis process to include one or all of the examples pointed out in this chapter?
- How will these processes help us to better tell our nonprofit story?
- Do we have a process for evaluating the work we do and is the community included?
- Do we have a strategy for communicating our work to the community, not just the funders?
- How can we utilize these tools to capture the results of our critical mentoring work?

Actions to Take

- *Develop a data plan.* Most nonprofit organizations have a semblance of a data plan, but it may not cover alternative approaches that include voices of youth or communities being served. It's worth revisiting this essential organizational process to ensure that it is in line with the critical work being done. This means looking beyond quantitative metrics and taking more time to make everyone in the organization a data collector. Take time during the annual retreat or other major meeting to revisit this and to develop a plan more in line with youth centrism and accountability to the community. Try using photovoice as an entry-level process. At the outset of a mentoring relationship, provide mentors with the tools they need to understand photovoice. Have them assign their protégés to take five pictures that tell the story of their lives, their families, and their neighborhoods. Also have them encourage their protégés to curate these photos via social media platforms. When they meet with their mentors again, they should be prepared to discuss their photos. Mentors should also have a photovoice project prepared to share; it is important to always be reciprocal. Programs can help to facilitate such an assignment by making it part of a program activity or event and providing space and time to share photographic narratives. This will also position the program to collect valuable data.
- *Engage in an annual empowerment evaluation.* Every year, the organization should take a close look at how the work has progressed. Youth, board members, staff, and community members need to engage in an ongoing process of looking at the mission, taking stock, and planning for the future. You don't have to employ an empowerment evaluator to facilitate the process yearly, but if you have funds, you can hire trained evaluators who can conduct an empowerment evaluation rather than one of the more traditional forms of evaluation. However, you can also conduct empowerment evaluations internally and on an ongoing basis, as with significant milestones. Reflection and connection to the community should be taking place on

a regular basis in a way that allows for the organization to be present and collaborative, grow, and gain strength.

- *Train every staff member to be a data collector.* Everyone in the organization must recognize the power of data and understand how important it is to collect it. It will not only help to shape your organization's narrative but also be instrumental in addressing the needs of your young people in their communities. Rather than focusing on deficits and metrics, recognizing the fact that valuable data exist in the places we least expect is important. This includes your young people. As suggested before, you can engage in a photovoice project as a starter with your protégés and show them that their stories are valuable treasures filled with relevant information. They will learn the power of their voice and feel free to utilize it in ways that will benefit the work tremendously. Every organization has a data person, someone who already leans in the "researcher" direction. Send that person to be trained in community, narrative, and qualitative research practices and have them teach other members of the organization. Utilize Payne and Brown's (2010) concept of street PAR and engage community members in a research task force that provides them with valuable research skills and then engages them in a process of identifying, studying, and addressing a community concern (Payne & Brown, 2010).
- *Focus on what is being done well in the community and build on it.* Rework your needs statements. Look to identify what is going well within the communities you serve and find ways to partner and support that work. Collaboration is a new and emerging nonprofit priority, more now than ever because of the way funders gauge impact. Don't be too eager to partner with other major organizations if you already are one; instead, consider helping to build the capacity of a smaller and similar organization. As you contribute to building their capacity, they will inform your work in ways that will make you more relevant and useful to the community.
- *Find innovative ways to share the data you capture with communities and stakeholders.* Annual reports are great, but we live in a technological information-sharing world that

allows many ways to share the excellent work being done. Infographics, social media, and online video platforms mean that we can tell stories and engage supporters en masse. Utilize these tools to make information easily consumable and available to a wide array of audiences. While you may be more inclined to use these tools outside of your communities, don't forget that these methods won't work for everyone. If it's a better idea to utilize a town hall, or a meet and greet, or a backyard BBQ to engage your community, then do so and share your work there.

This chapter may seem far from the discussion of mentoring and youth development work that preceded it, but it isn't. From the outset I have challenged mentoring and youth development organizations to rethink mentoring and youth development work, to shift paradigms, to turn things upside down. This chapter is in that same vein. While it does provide organizations with ways to "legitimize" critical mentoring work with research, it is also about developing our youth. As we work in these processes alongside our youth, we are modeling ways to engage, to do research, and to build a credible business structure. We are, in essence, doing the mentoring and youth development work we tout and providing our young people with valuable resources and experiences that they can use in schools and their future careers (e.g., as social entrepreneurs, corporate heads, and educational leaders). Many of us could only have hoped that we had as much research and organizational experience before entering the work field as youth engaged in critical mentoring organizations. At the Youth Mentoring Action Network we call this "growing our own" because our young people are at the center of every aspect of our social entrepreneurial project, learning everything about the organization and gaining skills and resume credit far beyond those of most of their peers.

We must find alternative ways to define and share our work. We must share the work with folks we typically wouldn't, we must add value to the less visible but more nuanced work in which we engage, and we must do it in responsible ways that center the voices and knowledge of the young people we serve.

6

A COLLECTIVE CALL TO
ACTION

This is your call to action. Mentoring has a new role to play
in helping young people to transform communities and,
ultimately, the world. The problem has and continues to be
that much of the work in which mentoring and youth development
organizations engage is deficit based; tokenized; and predicated on the
suffering of Black, Brown, queer, and othered bodies. Underlying many
organizational missions is the acknowledgment that there has been a
persistent and systematic destruction of families and communities and
that state-sanctioned and other forces have consistently undermined
and pervasively attacked progress for particular youths. Furthermore,
some of the same structures that harm communities in the first place
have set up other apparatuses, in the form of philanthropic work, to
profit from that suffering. In essence, while law, policy, and sociocultural
factors marginalize these young bodies, they also presume to fund the
"fixing" of their damage. This cyclical process in which philanthropy
benefits from the destruction of the marginalized and minoritized is at
best a conflict of interest and at worst a dubious and insidious ploy. As
daunting as that statement may seem, I do not believe that many of the
folks inside these mentoring and youth development organizations are
engaged in community service with this in mind. I believe that the heart
of nonprofit and community work is the hope that communities and

the people within them can be healed by sincere investments of time, collaboration, and resources. This belief is affirmed by the countless organizations who are working to reframe narratives, shift patterns, and transform communities. However, the understanding that many of the "problems" we are attempting to address are rooted in systemic, structural, ubiquitous ways of doing business means we should be explicit about how we engage in our work and mindful not to reproduce the same systems we claim to address. That's a tall order, but necessary for critical mentoring work. Our young people are savvy—they get it, they see the bigger picture, even when we cannot and are failing to appeal to them because we are running the same programs, mouthing the same slogans, and maintaining the same frameworks. Radical change must occur.

Mentoring, as an age-old practice steeped in tradition, is evolving rapidly and must cease to be the practice adults want it to be and become the practice young people need it to be. To radically resist timeworn institutions, to reimagine antiquated spaces, to transform the ways nonprofit business is done, mentoring must become the new field of critical inquiry and praxis. It is too important to be missed, too essential to be relegated to "other folks," too necessary to be ignored. Every single youth deserves to have a caring and supportive mentor willing to pull up his or her sleeves and partner in this work. And given the nature of the toxic contexts in which marginalized and minoritized youth exist, mentoring processes that support the positive development of racial identity and the creation of liberatory frameworks are what young people require.

If not us, then who? Critical mentoring must be at once reciprocal, collaborative, participatory, emancipatory, and transformative. It must become the foundation that the youth movement rests on and not because youth need adults, but because adults need youth. Adults need alternate ways of thinking and viewing the world; we need innovative ideas and the guts to carry them out; we need spring in our step, the creativity that comes from unapologetic boldness, and the fervor of youth. Critical mentoring begs us to shift the paradigm, to change it up, to challenge what was and to create what will be. Critical mentoring is for everybody. It is not limited to schools or community programs; it is about engaging entire communities in the work of advocating for and supporting our young people. Each might have their youth population, their immediate context, but the society in which our young people and we relate still needs to be changed. Critical mentoring is not relegated to community programs. It is for anyone doing mentoring and youth development work. As our young people move through K–12 schools, in and out of communities, and onto college campuses the support we offer them must be real and relevant. Each of us has to participate, and each of us must understand that this is not about helping our young people adjust to toxicity; this work is about clearing the air and purifying the water so that we can all breathe and drink.

For Community Programs

Mentoring and youth development programs working within communities are well positioned to utilize the tools suggested in this book. You are or should be well aware of the landscape as well as the need for this particular type of work. Lead the charge, make critical mentoring central to your work, and be the example for other community-based nonprofits and programs that aim to alter radically the trajectories of youth. Mentoring and youth development programs already see a pressing need to help youth; our missions and program goals say so. What is necessary is a more nuanced way of understanding those needs as well as a more innovative approach to addressing them. As mentioned before, the work of community programs seeking to be critical is to begin to address pervasive and systemic issues facing marginalized and minoritized youth within the context of communities, larger society, and the globe while being funded by many of the same entities who have created these problems in the first place. Community programs must see their efforts as ground level, which requires a sense of who the young people in those communities are, what issues are pressing for them, and how your funding can be utilized to address these problems in the most efficient ways. The purpose is to be intentional about concentrating your efforts on actually solving problems alongside young people. Critical mentoring means engaging with young people and in ways that might make us uncomfortable, that might make us worry we are working ourselves out of jobs. While I agree that working to effect actual change might make some people feel uncomfortable about the future of their programs, it is necessary for the future of our young people and necessary for generations to come. We will always have a youth population to mentor, but we should not always have to mentor them through racist, classist, sexist, and ableist structures.

Community programs should use this book as a starting point. It should be the impetus for discussions about how to make the work you are doing relevant to those you serve and how to "do" mentoring in ways that begin to address the myriad structural problems we know exist but have trouble getting at with the processes we currently have. Community programs also have the opportunity to work alongside one another in ways that are innovative and collaborative rather than competitive and individualistic. Our digital society has reframed the notion of community so that community centers, spaces that were physically present, where young people could go, and access services are dwindling. We have left very few youth-centric spaces for young people to congregate and interact. This is not to say that the digital shift is an entirely bad one, just that community service organizations need to consider this lack of physical presence as they endeavor to do critical mentoring work. If you are operating in spaces that don't center youth, have none or very few youth-centric spaces, and you are trying to center and value human connection and interactivity, physical space is necessary. If you are operating in communities where poverty has displaced community spaces for young people and you are working to bring programming that requires physical space, these issues become ones you must tackle alongside your young people to find ways of rebuilding the community and providing these physical spaces once again. Still, community programs cannot pretend to operate in an isolated fashion. Community programs must build coalitions with K–12 schools, colleges and universities, as well as local businesses and corporations and must advocate for creating wraparound support and opportunities for young people. Community programs should again become the center of youth innovation, providing opportunities for young people to express themselves, develop themselves, and create anew.

Community programs have the responsibility to engage in mentoring processes that move beyond holding young people accountable to adults and toward holding adults accountable to young people. What good is it to ask the youth you are mentoring to perform well in school if the school doesn't meet that young person's needs? When do mentors learn to advocate for their protégés, to be part of holding schools accountable for providing the education and support young people need to thrive? Community-based mentoring, because it operates outside of schools, has to be a space for young people to name the trauma they might be experiencing in schools. It has to be a space for young people to engage in instructional processes that don't fall back on traditional ways of schooling; it has to be about connecting them to their communities and providing opportunities for that community to instruct them. Community-based mentoring can't be solely about men teaching young men how to tie ties; it can't be solely about coming in for a "day of mentoring" and then moving on to the next project; it can't be solely about photo opportunities, big checks, and pseudocollaborations. Community-based mentoring that is critical has to be about concentrated efforts to offer youth-centric spaces that are safe, trauma-free platforms for free expression and building. Community-based programs have a responsibility to engage in critical mentoring; they must, if operating in the community, partner with the community to create thriving and sustainable pathways for the young people they serve. No more profiting on "need" without engaging in the critical work required to actually address the need, even better, eradicate the need. No more fully funded budgets for processes that further marginalize young people or support the structures that marginalize them. No more profit from the pain our young people experience. Do the critical work or make room for someone who will.

For K–12 Schools

As locally controlled funding becomes available to K–12 schools, funding specifically designated to addressing marginalized and minoritized youth, schools have begun to implement school-based mentoring programs to provide wraparound services and support. However, I have seen schools undermine this attempt by implementing poorly planned and less than effective mentoring programs that are little more than tutoring opportunities. Schools should see this text as a way to begin engaging in mentoring processes that not only make the difference for the young people in their schools but also radically change the way schools operate for young people. Critical mentoring requires that we work alongside young people, that we create youth-centric spaces;

schools often have a long way to go in doing this. Many of the school-based programs I have seen focus on providing students with mentors who will tutor them, help them improve academically, raise test scores, and increase attendance. Although we understand that mentoring programs organized on evidence-based practices can contribute to improvement in these areas, how does this approach help to change schools for the young people within them? What this method does is ask students to adapt to often dysfunctional schools.

The Youth Mentoring Action Network is a hybrid of community- and school-based mentoring, and we have lots of conversations about topics such as grades, attendance, and behavior with the young people with whom we work. A critical mentor will recognize immediately that young people often have real reasons for not performing well in school. Even reasons adults often dismiss or consider ridiculous aren't to be discounted because they inform our understanding of school systems. Critical mentoring in schools requires that mentors see beyond young people's grades or behavior and connect with them for what they bring beyond the often rigid and limited constructions of academic performance. Critical mentoring also means recognizing that schools, as microcosms of society, are complicit in problematizing and pushing out marginalized and minoritized youth. The result of this is that many of those mentoring conversations must move beyond attempting to fix the youth and into fixing their school context. My current protégé is a young Black female. She is often viewed as talkative, lackadaisical, not achieving at her full potential. In our weekly meetings, we spend lots of time talking about intellectual pursuits without ever mentioning "school performance." Had my sole focus as her mentor been looking at my protégé's grades I would never have understood that she is, in fact, a brilliant and budding engineer. She has an unbelievable knack for electronics and we often discuss possible building projects. Once I gave her three circuit board sequencers to take home and experiment with. She returned with a complete understanding of how to operate them, connect them to other devices, utilize them as controllers, and even build one of her own. My responsibility as a critical mentor is to understand why my protégé's talents are so underrecognized and undervalued by her school and then to help her thrive in ways that are necessary for her. It is also to help her family understand this issue so as not to allow the school's deficit-based view of my protégé to mar her family's understanding of her unique talents. Schools and mentors miss the mark when they focus on "fixing" protégés so that they adapt to schools. I fully understand the realist perspective that grades matter, that test scores matter, and that the real world requires our young people adjust. However, I disagree that it is more important to tell a brilliant youth to adapt and assimilate than work alongside that young person to alter systems and help them function better for young people in the long run. Again, critical mentoring is about shifting paradigms. Mentoring has been a sort of accomplice for dysfunctional school systems, always emphasizing what young people need to do to change rather than asking schools to change and provide for young people.

Schools implementing mentoring programs must consider the responsibility they have to ensure that young people are fully supported and engaged at every level. Most important, schools implementing mentoring programs must be sure to recruit and train adults who will operate as mentors, not as authoritarians. The challenge for teachers who also try to mentor is that they confuse their roles as educators, which are typically authoritarian, with their roles as mentors, which are not. Mentoring relationships are not forged in moments of finger wagging, judging, and bossing. Mentoring relationships are formed through understanding, openness, and mutual respect. To do critical mentoring work in schools means to renegotiate spaces so that protégés can speak openly about their experiences, be vulnerable enough to ask for help, and feel free to challenge what they think is wrong without being chastised. This is not to say that young people don't require guidance; of course they do, but they don't require it in the authoritarian "speak when spoken to" ways that schools often utilize. Critical mentoring in schools also means having hard conversations, engaging in reflective processes that don't always make us feel good. Sometimes what we see through the eyes and voices of our young people will be appalling, will force us to reconcile with truths we may not wish to face. But this work is necessary for us to move in a direction of clearing the air and purifying the water. How can we act to do something we don't recognize? Many of us have assimilated, have adjusted to breathing toxic air and drinking toxic water. We often become educators or work in schools because we excel at it. We become quite good at surviving despite the toxicity and have even evolved in ways that allow us to navigate without concern. Critical mentoring in schools means recognizing this fact, checking it, and working alongside young people to alter it. In employing critical mentoring, original goals such as improving grades and attendance are often accomplished. However, now both mentor and protégé have gained a critical consciousness or more critical awareness and are both engaged in making change.

Schools, too, have a responsibility to reach out to the community, to partner with community organizations, colleges and universities, and businesses. Young people should know that schools are doing work that will support them beyond their walls, that they are creating opportunities that will help them to thrive later on in life. The checks-and-balances process includes schools as well. Don't partner with or encourage young people to work with community organizations that aren't engaging in critical work. Schools are often key points of information dissemination for community programs and colleges; schools should work with like-minded programs and ensure that only those programs that are serving young people well are provided with opportunities to connect with young people. Schools should also connect with local mentoring organizations, specifically those doing critical work, to receive training for campus mentors and help teachers to understand the differences between mentoring and teaching. Our young people spend the majority of their time in school, so it is the responsibility of our schools to foster critical mentorships so that youth are fully supported from the time they first enter school to the time they leave.

For Colleges and Universities

Higher education institutions also have been working to engage a growing group of marginalized and minoritized youth coming onto their campuses. As student services folks set up mentoring programs to go about providing support, they should be well aware of the critical mentoring concept as well as how to implement it in student services programs. Colleges and universities have a unique role to play in critical mentoring processes because marginalized and minoritized students often arrive at these campuses believing that they have somehow moved past many of the challenges they have had with the debilitating structures we've been discussing. They are often shocked and devastated when they discover that they must still work to have their humanity recognized, that inequity is still very entrenched in higher education spaces, that they may have an even harder time acquiring mentors at this level. They have made it through high school and into college, which for most young people is a celebrated stop en route to their dream, but they still require mentoring relationships to help them move to their next levels.

Colleges and universities typically house these programs under the auspices of admissions or students services, both of which have the responsibility of recruiting, maintaining, and supporting every young person on campus. But what does that look like in the context of your campus, its history, its systems? Again, if the goal is to create a mentoring program that will help minoritized and marginalized youth adapt to a college campus rooted in inequitable structures, rather than a mentoring program that provides support and works to change structures, you are doing more harm than good. It is important to consider processes on your campus that create challenges for minoritized and marginalized youth and to create a critical mentoring program that supports them in their critique and challenge of those systems and works with them to change it. Rather than operating from the perspective that youth of color have a hard time adjusting to the campus and wanting to pair them with a mentor who can show them how to navigate, operate from the perspective that these youth have something unique to offer the campus and that they require resources and opportunities to illustrate that. Steer away from using program titles that further minoritize and marginalize these young people. If the title of your program emphasizes the otherness of the protégés or participants, it might make it unattractive to those being served by it and, worse, exacerbate the marginalization they are already experiencing. It isn't an empowering experience to join a program that tells you via its title, "You don't belong here so we are going to fix you so you can belong."

Mentoring programs on college and university campuses have categorical responsibilities to support young people with the resources and supports they will need to further their education and careers. Moving beyond meetings and activities, colleges and universities need to establish systems whereby these young people can be matched with staff and faculty members who can help them to connect to internships, paid job opportunities, career development, academic publishing opportunities, anything that their counterparts may be receiving more easily and without reservation. A Wharton School study noted that women and ethnic minorities have a much harder time engaging faculty in mentoring processes than do their White and male counterparts (Milkman, Akinola, & Chugh, 2015). The study revealed that students with female or ethnic names were less likely to receive a response or a positive response when contacting faculty via e-mail about an opportunity to sit down and talk (Milkman et al., 2015). This finding illustrates the need for institutions to explicitly create pathways or systems for mentoring opportunities for minoritized and marginalized youth. It means actively recruiting and training staff and faculty to engage in these mentoring relationships, and it might also mean incentivizing the staff and faculty who participate. It should also be noted that staff and faculty of color are almost always engaged in these processes already by default and that the extra time and resources they provide these students tend to go unrecognized in institutional ways that matter such as promotion and tenure.

In establishing peer-to-peer mentoring on college campuses, these programs need to recruit diverse student populations to serve as mentors and train them to understand that their mentoring must be active, not passive, and be centered in advocacy. Predominantly White college campuses may have trouble recruiting diversely to begin with, and that will be the initial sign that these campuses have even more responsibility to work to clear the air and purify the water. Be sure the programs on campus have solid training curriculums that focus on not only evidence-based mentoring strategies but also cultural relevance and critical issues. Participants need to engage in discussions about what the campus, society, and the larger world looks like and is for marginalized and minoritized youth. These trainings should not be conducted in comfortable isolation; they should include the very voices of the people the program seeks to serve. Don't forget the mantra "not about us without us." As college campuses deal with trying to increase diversity on their campuses as well as meet the needs of their young people who are minoritized and marginalized, critical mentoring provides some answers. It is a way to establish a permanent, institutional structure that will welcome young people, give them the space and support they require to thrive, and become an incubator for transformation on the campus.

In the same way community organizations and K–12 schools should engage in collaborative partnerships, so should colleges and universities. Partner with local high schools to provide pipelines for young people to your campuses. Work with community organizations to establish programs that expose young people to college campuses and classrooms. Bring in community organizations doing critical mentoring work to help train your staff, faculty, and student mentors, and establish joint events that bring community members together to find ways to address issues and needs. Colleges and universities must become more community centric; they must earn the funding they receive to educate the community.

For Researchers

Although I have not directly addressed researchers in this text, it is important to note that mentoring and youth researchers have a responsibility to move the critical mentoring agenda forward as well. The way we study mentoring, the body of mentoring work, requires vicissitude. Mentoring research, although utilizing race, ethnicity, class, gender, and sexuality for marketing and surface exploration, does not give these issues the critical examination they deserve. In fact, much of the mentoring research focuses on the nature of relationships, outcomes of the relationships, and evaluation metrics bent on justifying the existence of mentoring programs. Some mentoring researchers have ventured down the path of more critical work; David DuBois, Bernadette Sánchez, and Noelle Hurd are just a few of them. However, the result of a limited focus in mentoring research is that many questions and issues around race, ethnicity, class, gender, and sexuality, especially those we are often most uncomfortable with, go unexplored. Why has the face of mentoring been predominantly White, showcasing White mentors with protégés of color? Why has mentoring rested on deficit-based notions of communities and youth of color? How does that pathology influence what youth are likely to engage in those relationships, who they expect to mentor them, and what they expect from that mentor? Are naturally occurring mentoring relationships, which the research suggests are harder to track, a result of this pathology, at least in part? How do program goals, as measured by evaluation metrics, serve the needs of the community, not just the needs of the funders? And so on. Critical mentoring seeks to move mentoring research into a larger discourse around the critical examination of race, ethnicity, class, gender, and sexuality as they pertain to mentoring. Critical mentoring asks us to challenge deficit-based notions in our research, those of protégés, limited metrics that ignore metanarratives and protégé adaptation to dominant ideologies.

Critical mentoring requests that researchers utilize critical frameworks such as critical race theory and critical pedagogy for the analysis of mentoring relationships, mentoring outcomes, programmatic structures, and outcomes. In addition, critical mentoring asks us to rethink the way we evaluate mentoring programs. We need to move beyond standard evaluative strategy and utilize evaluative methods that empower protégés and highlight programmatic outcomes beyond statistical ones, such as empowerment evaluation and photovoice. Critical mentoring begs us to engage in new and more critical forms of research.

For Leaders

The nuts and bolts of critical mentoring, even as it progresses, are only part of solid critical community work. Leadership is the key to making it all come together. Without critically engaged, youth-centric, and community-based leaders, much of this work will be watered down and tokenized. As this book has emphasized, the word *leadership* must not be viewed in antiquated and traditional ways. It is not meant to point to a sole figure or figurehead who dictates what the rest of the people within an organization must do. In this context, leadership means folks who are at the edges of critical thought, who are willing to challenge and defend for the sake of young people. Leadership means being uncompromising in the desire to make a radical change and prepared to challenge the status quo of nonprofit business in communities that are marginalized and minoritized. And this leadership is necessary. I have suggested time and again that we have to rethink and innovate, and these initial steps are the work of community leaders who will begin to "talk back," to help shift the trend of philanthropic funding and make connections between and among communities, nonprofits, K–12 schools, and colleges and universities.

It is the responsibility of action and thought leaders reading this book to begin doing the pushing inside of institutions that is required for people to move. Begin asking questions about how and why things are done the way they are, start forming coalitions of people who are willing to engage in more critical work, and set up conferences and symposiums to provide space for people to gather and plan. Leaders have vision, and more often than not, that vision is necessary to provide the impetus to move forward. Leaders should be looking for ways to center youth in their work as much as possible. You may be the only person who begins bringing protégés to the board meetings, but that modeling is necessary if making the argument that youth should be sitting on nonprofit boards. You may be the only one who has a clear idea of what a birth-to-college pipeline looks like for the youth in your community; it requires unmitigated outspokenness and leadership to begin moving other folks in the same direction. Leaders must utilize critical mentoring to shift the ways organizations think, to change the ways communities are centered in the conversation, to see the bigger picture and begin influencing systems in a manner that means more results for our young people. Peter Drucker (1990) noted that "in the non-profit agency, mediocrity in leadership shows up almost immediately. . . . You can't be satisfied in non-profit organizations with doing adequately as a leader. You have to do exceptionally well, because your agency is committed to a cause" (p. 17). Leaders in the mentoring movement must see critical mentoring as the difference between mediocrity and doing exceptionally well by our youth. That difference will not only change organizations but also alter funding patterns and begin to create real and substantive opportunities for young people.

Getting the Work Done

The idea that each and every one of us benefits from serving these young people is not lost on me, and it won't be lost on them. But there is a distinct difference between being compensated for the work we do and taking advantage of a system that rewards token work. As Larry Thomas of the Thomas Mentor Leadership Academy says, "I hope part of the change is for organizations and individuals to stop pimping our youth for their advantage" (personal communication, June 2016). We must see to it that the benefits we receive are not undeserved, that we are doing all we can to ensure that our young people are provided with the resources they need to become successful. And, most important, we must be careful not to reproduce the very same systems we know are harming young people. The mentoring work that we do should be about moving all of us forward. It is important to ask ourselves what mentoring looks like in the age of Black Lives Matter, in the age of mass incarceration, in the age of fully funded wars and crumbling schools. We must ask ourselves what mentoring means in the context of the school-to-prison pipeline, respectability politics, or nonprofit businesses that garner more profits and benefits than they provide to youth.

We must challenge the notion that only some youth need mentors, that suburban youth are fine whereas urban youth are a mess, and that we must concentrate our efforts in only one space. We must challenge the falsehood that Black boys are more important or need more help than Black girls, that Latino youth aren't "of color," that heterosexual youth are more important than queer youth, that the White supremacy rooted in all of it doesn't hurt every single young person everywhere. Let's stop saying that liberation and politics isn't part of what we do as mentors. Let's steer away from ideas that keep mentors on the sidelines and outside the scope of movements and liberatory processes. The truth is we know that young people who are supported by adults, engaged in communities, and given educational opportunities are the best chance we have at making a societal impact. If we don't invest in them, there will be no us.

Crucial to this collective action is the issue of professional development training. Every entity doing mentoring and youth development work must invest in training that includes a critical examination of race, ethnicity, class, gender, sexuality, and ability. It cannot be negotiated and is the beginning of dialogue and subsequently action. A person whose lived experiences can speak to a number of these issues should facilitate this training and everyone within the organization should be required to attend. In addition, this training cannot be a onetime experience; it must be part of a yearly process that is kept in motion by internal processing and dialoguing throughout the year. Only in open, reflective, and informative spaces can people within organizations begin piecing critical mentoring praxis together. It requires critical interrogation of self, society, and organization, making facilitated trainings essential.

This text is a call to action. It is a throwing down of the gauntlet, a challenge to rethink how mentoring works, to look at how we can support forward-thinking movements, and to ask us to participate in the youth innovation happening globally. This text is another aspect of the new mentoring movement, a way to move us forward, a way for us to join the call for change happening everywhere, a way for adults to join young people as they rally for transformation, for change. Critical mentoring is a beginning, and it's an evolving concept. This text is an invitation to make additions, to build on it, to elevate it, to remix it—anything to make us better for our young people.

SUGGESTED READINGS

Andrews, M., Squire, C., & Tamboukou, M. (Eds.). (2008). *Doing narrative research*. Thousand Oaks, CA: Sage.
Complete with theoretical underpinnings and steps for coding and analysis, this straightforward and thorough guide on how to conduct narrative research provides all that is needed to collect stories for your organization.

Coates, T.-N. (2015). *Between the world and me*. New York, NY: Spiegel & Grau.
Coates's book, written in the form of a letter to his son, provides gripping, realistic, and detailed substance. He expounds on the issue of race in America in a personalized and vulnerable way. This text offers those mentoring youth of color, particularly boys and young men, the insight they need to understand the myriad complexities of being racialized in America.

Cooperrider, D. L., Whitney, D., & Stavros, J. M. (2008). *Appreciative inquiry handbook: For leaders of change* (2nd ed.). Brunswick, OH: Crown Custom Publishing.
This accessible and informative handbook outlines the theoretical and practical components of appreciative inquiry. Organizations looking to utilize the strategy will find that this handbook provides the relevant processes for implementing appreciative inquiry projects within programs and organizations.

Daneshzadeh, A., Washington, A., & Cumi, K. (in press). Standing in solidarity with Black girls to dismantle the school-to-prison pipeline. In R. Elmesky, C. Yeakey, & O. Marcucci (Eds.), *The power of resistance: Culture, ideology and social reproduction in global contexts*. St. Louis, MO: Emerald Press.

Focusing on using hip-hop to help young Black girls in schools, this book chapter is an excellent example of how hip-hop music can be used therapeutically, but also in defiance of prohibitive, racialized, and gendered school structures. This is particularly important to read for mentoring programs operating in schools.

Emdin, C. (2016). *For white folks who teach in the hood and the rest of ya'll too.* Boston, MA: Beacon Press.

Emdin provides instruction and advice for dealing with marginalized and minoritized youth. The same ideas posited in this text are applicable to mentoring and youth development programs operating in similar contexts. The book also speaks to effective ways to connect with new youth, no matter the context, given the savvy and cosmopolitan ways in which contemporary youth behave.

Fetterman, D., & Wandersman, A. (2007). Empowerment evaluation: Yesterday, today, and tomorrow. *American Journal of Evaluation, 28*(2), 179–198. http://doi.org/10.1177/1098214007301350

Like the handbook on appreciative inquiry listed previously, this article on empowerment evaluation provides the base needed to begin utilizing it in mentoring and youth development organizations. The text provides real-life and organization-based examples of how it has been employed and is a go-to guide for immediate implementation. Empowerment evaluation can be integrated into regular processes throughout the program year, the findings can be included in the internal annual report, and they can also inform larger evaluation processes in which organizations participate.

Guide to mentoring boys and young men of color. (2016). Retrieved from www.mentoring.org/new-site/wp-content/uploads/2016/05/Guide-to-Mentoring-BYMOC.pdf

The My Brother's Keeper movement has increased the attention on boys and young men of color. Subsequently, there have been calls for mentoring standards to include processes that would help mentoring and youth development programs to better serve this population. This newly developed guide, put out by MENTOR and My Brother's Keeper, provides a set of standards for programs working with boys and young men of color. It is packed with important information regarding the context of these youth and guidance for how to better mentor them.

Lamont Hill, M. (2016). *Nobody: Casualties of America's war on the vulnerable, from Ferguson to Flint and beyond.* New York, NY: Atria Books.

This phenomenal text takes the time to explain and describe the context of toxicity referred to in this book. Lamont Hill not only tells the story of contemporary state-sanctioned killings, beatings, and so forth, but also takes the time to describe the history, the economical, the political, the class, and the race contexts that lead up to and surround these incidences. With uncanny clarity, this text will help mentors to understand the "nobodyness" of their protégés in ways others have yet to describe.

Mirra, N., Garcia, A., & Morrell, E. (2015). *Doing youth participatory action research.* New York, NY: Routledge.

This text provides the theoretical underpinnings of youth participatory action research (YPAR), examples of YPAR at work, and reflections on the YPAR process. Centering on a real-life project undertaken by the authors, this book informs the implementation of YPAR within mentoring and youth development organizations. Included are the steps required for YPAR and student explanations of YPAR work.

Section 20. Implementing photovoice in your community. (2016). *Community Tool Box.* Retrieved from http://ctb.ku.edu/en/table-of-contents/assessment/assessing-community-needs-and-resources/photovoice/main

The Community Tool Box website provides a wealth of valuable information for building communities. The photovoice section details the process for implementing photovoice projects within communities, which makes it most appropriate for mentoring and youth development programs. Examples of community-based photovoice projects are linked to the site, as are examples of suggested readings on the topic.

REFERENCES

About the Black Lives Matter network. (n.d.). Retrieved from http://blacklivesmatter.com/about/

Anderson, C., & Dixson, A. (2016). Down by the riverside: A CRT perspective on education reform in two river cities. *Urban Education*, *51*(4), 363–389.

Andrews, M., Squire, C., & Tamboukou, M. (Eds.). (2008). *Doing narrative research*. Thousand Oaks, CA: Sage.

Baker, D. B., & Maguire, C. P. (2005). Mentoring in historical perspective. In D. L. DuBois & M. J. Karcher (Eds.), *Handbook of youth mentoring* (pp. 14–29). Thousand Oaks, CA: Sage.

Black, D. S., Grenard, J. L., Sussman, S., & Rohrbach, L. A. (2010). The influence of school-based natural mentoring relationships on school attachment and subsequent adolescent risk behaviors. *Health Education Research*, *25*(5), 892–902. http://doi.org/10.1093/her/cyq040

Bryant, A., & Payne, Y. (2013). Evaluating the impact of community-based learning: Participatory action research as a model for inside-out. In S. W. Davis & B. S. Roswell (Eds.), *Turning teaching inside out: A pedagogy of transformation for community-based education* (pp. 227–239). New York, NY: Palgrave Macmillan US. http://doi.org/10.1057/9781137331021_23

Coates, T.-N. (2015). *Between the world and me*. New York, NY: Spiegel & Grau.

Cohen, C. J. (2009). Black Youth Project [dataset]. Chicago, Il: University of Chicago. *Center for the Study of Race, Politics and Culture*. Retrieved from www.blackyouthproject.com

Cooperrider, D. L., Whitney, D., & Stavros, J. M. (2008). *Appreciative inquiry handbook: For leaders of change* (2nd ed.). Brunswick, OH: Crown Custom Publishing.

Crenshaw, K. (1989). Demarginalizing the intersection of race and sex: A Black feminist critique of antidiscrimination doctrine, feminist theory and antiracist politics. *University of Chicago Legal Forum, 1989*(1), article 8. Retrieved from http://chicagounbound.uchicago.edu/uclf/vol1989/iss1/8

Daneshzadeh, A., Washington, A., & Cumi, K. (in press). Standing in solidarity with Black girls to dismantle the school-to-prison pipeline. In R. Elmesky, C. Yeakey, & O. Marcucci (Eds.), *The power of resistance: Culture, ideology and social reproduction in global contexts*. St. Louis, MO: Emerald Press.

Delgado, R., & Stefancic, J. (2012). *Critical race theory: An introduction*. New York, NY: New York University Press.

Dove, S. (2015). Rumble Young Man Rumble. In *Keynote Address*. Louisville, KY.

Drucker, P. (1990). *Managing the nonprofit organization*. New York, NY: HarperCollins.

DuBois, D. L., Holloway, B. E., Valentine, J. C., & Cooper, H. (2002). Effectiveness of mentoring programs for youth: A meta-analytic review. *American Journal of Community Psychology, 30*(2), 157–197.

DuBois, D. L., & Karcher, M. J. (2014). Youth mentoring in contemporary perspective. In D. L. DuBois & M. J. Karcher (Eds.), *Handbook of youth mentoring* (2nd ed., pp. 3–13). Thousand Oaks, CA: Sage.

DuBois, D. L., Portillo, N., Rhodes, J. E., Silverthorn, N., & Valentine, J. C. (2011). How effective are mentoring programs for youth? A systematic assessment of the evidence. *Psychological Science in the Public Interest, 12*(2), 57–91.

Dumas, M. J. (2016). "Be Real Black for Me": Imagining BlackCrit in Education. *Urban Education*, 42085916628611.

Edelman, M. W. (1999). *Lanterns: A memoir of mentors*. New York, NY: HarperCollins.

Emdin, C. (2016a). *For white folks who teach in the hood and the rest of ya'll too*. Boston, MA: Beacon Press.

Emdin, C. (2016b, March). How can white teachers do better by urban kids of color? *ColorLines*. Retrieved from http://www.colorlines.com/articles/how-can-white-teachers-do-better-urban-kids-color

Fetterman, D., & Wandersman, A. (2007). Empowerment evaluation: Yesterday, today, and tomorrow. *American Journal of Evaluation, 28*(2), 179–198. http://doi.org/10.1177/1098214007301350

Fetterman, D., Kaftarian, S., & Wandersman, A. (2015). *Empowerment evaluation: Knowledge and tools for self assessment, evaluation capcity building, and accountability*. Thousand Oaks: Sage Publications.

Foundation Center. (2015). *Quantifying hope: Philanthropic support for Black men and boys*. Retrieved from http://bmafunders.org/wp-content/uploads/2015/04/quantifying-hope-web-final.pdf

Freire, P. (1970). *Pedagogy of the oppressed*. New York, NY: Continuum.

Gaddis, S. M. (2012). What's in a relationship? An examination of social capital, race and class in mentoring relationships. *Social Forces, 90*(4), 1237–1269.

Garringer, M., Kupersmidt, J., Rhodes, J. E., Stelter, R., & Tai, T. (2015). *Elements of effective practice for mentoring.* Retrieved from http://www .mentoring.org/new-site/wp-content/uploads/2016/01/Final_Elements_ Publication_Fourth.pdf

Gillborn, D., Rollock, N., Vincent, C., & Ball, S. J. (2012). "You got a pass, so what more do you want?": Race, class and gender intersections in the educational experiences of the Black middle class. *Race Ethnicity and Education,* 15(1), 1211–39. http://doi.org/10.1080/13613324.2012.638869

Goings, R. (2015). The lion tells his side of the (counter) story: A Black male educator's autoethnographic account. *Journal of African American Males in Education,* 6(1), 91–105.

Guide to mentoring boys and young men of color. (2016). Retrieved from http:// www.mentoring.org/new-site/wp-content/uploads/2016/05/Guide-to-Mentoring-BYMOC.pdf

Harris, F. C. (2014). The rise of respectability politics. *Dissent,* 61(1), 33–37.

Hurd, N. M., Sánchez, B., Zimmerman, M. A., & Caldwell, C. H. (2012). Natural mentors, racial identity, and educational attainment among African American adolescents: Exploring pathways to success. *Child Development,* 83(4), 1196–1212. http://doi.org/10.1111/j.1467-8624.2012.01769.x

Hurd, N. M., & Sellers, R. M. (2013). Black adolescents' relationships with natural mentors: Associations with academic engagement via social and emotional development. *Cultural Diversity and Ethnic Minority Psychology,* 19(1), 76–85.

Keller, T. E. (2010). Youth mentoring: Theoretical and methodological issues. In T. D. Allen & L. T. Eby (Eds.), *The Blackwell handbook of mentoring: A multiple perspectives approach* (pp. 23–47). Malden, MA: Blackwell Publishing.

Kohnen, M. (2015). *Queer representaton, visibility, and race in American film and television.* London: Routledge.

Ladson-Billings, G. (1995a). But that's just good teaching! The case for culturally relevant pedagogy. *Theory Into Practice,* 34(3), 159–165.

Ladson-Billings, G. (1995b). *The dreamkeepers: Successful teachers of African American children.* San Francisco, CA: Jossey-Bass.

Ladson-Billings, G., & Tate, W. F. (1995). Toward a critical race theory of education. *Teachers College Record,* 97(1), 47–68.

Lamont Hill, M. (2016). *Nobody: Casualties of America's war on the vulnerable from Ferguson to Flint and beyond.* New York, NY: Atria Books.

Love, B. (in press). "She has a real connection with them": Reimagining and expanding our definitions of Black masculinity and mentoring in education through female masculinity.

McIntyre, A. (2008). *Participatory action research.* Thousand Oaks, CA: Sage.

McTaggart, R. (2001). Guiding principles for participatory action research. In C. F. Conrad, J. G. Haworth, & L. R. Lattuca (Eds.), *Research in higher education: Expanding perspectives* (2nd ed., pp. 263–274). Boston, MA: Pearson.

Milkman, K. L., Akinola, M., & Chugh, D. (2015). What happens before? A field experiment exploring how pay and representation differentially shape bias on the pathway into organizations. *Journal of Applied Psychology*, *100*(6), 1678–1712. http://dx.doi.org/10.1037/apl0000022

Mirra, N., Garcia, A., & Morrell, E. (2015). *Doing youth participatory action research*. New York, NY: Routledge.

My Brother's Keeper. (2016). *Guide to mentoring boys and young men of color*. Retrieved from http://www.mentoring.org/new-site/wp-content/uploads/2016/05/Guide-to-Mentoring-BYMOC.pdf

Paris, D. (2012). Culturally sustaining pedagogy: A needed change in stance, terminology, and practice. *Educational Researcher*, *41*(3), 93–97.

Park, H., Yoon, J., & Crosby, S. (2016). A pilot study of Big Brothers Big Sisters programs and youth development: An application of critical race theory. *Children and Youth Services Review*, *61*, 83–89.

Payne, Y. A., & Brown, T. M. (2010). The educational experience of street-life-oriented Black boys: How Black boys use street life as a site of resilience in high school. *Journal of Contemporary Justice*, *26*(3), 316–338.

Rhodes, J. (2015, May 18). The real mentoring gap—and what to do about it. *The Chronicle of Evidence-Based Mentoring*. Retrieved from http://chronicle.umbmentoring.org/the-real-mentoring-gap-what-to-do-about-it/

Rhodes, J. E., & DuBois, D. L. (2006). Understanding and facilitating the youth mentoring movement. *Social Policy Report, 20*(3), 3–19.

Roediger, D. (2006). *Working toward Whiteness: How America's immigrants became White: The strange journey from Ellis Island to the suburbs*. New York, NY: Basic Books.

Sánchez, B., Colón-Torres, Y., Feuer, R., Roundfield, K., & Berardi, L. (2014). Race, ethnicity, and culture in mentoring relationships. In D. L. DuBois & M. J. Karcher (Eds.), *Handbook of youth mentoring* (2nd ed., pp. 145–158). Thousand Oaks, CA: Sage.

Savin-Williams, R. (2005). *The new gay teenager*. Cambridge, MA: First Harvard University Press.

Section 20. Implementing photo voice in your community. (2016). *Community Tool Box*. Retrieved from http://ctb.ku.edu/en/table-of-contents/assessment/assessing-community-needs-and-resources/photovoice/main

Spencer, R. (2010). Naturally occurring mentoring relationships involving youth. In T. Allen & L. T. Eby (Eds.), *The Blackwell handbook of mentoring: A multiple perspectives approach* (pp. 97–117). Oxford: Blackwell.

Stanton-Salazar, R. D. (2011). A social capital framework for the study of institutional agents and their role in the empowerment of low-status students and youth. *Youth & Society, 43*(3), 1066–1109.

Stokely Carmichael Videos. (n.d.). Retrieved from http://www.history.com/topics/black-history/stokely-carmichael/videos/stokely-carmichael

Teranishi, R. (2005). *Black residential migration in California: Implications for higher education policy.* Retrieved from http://steinhardt.nyu.edu/scmsAdmin/uploads/005/841/RTT_RPIC.pdf

Valencia, R. R. (2010). *Dismantling contemporary deficit thinking.* New York, NY: Routledge.

Wang, C., & Burris, M. A. (1997). Photovoice: Concept, methodology, and use for participatory needs assessment. *Health Education & Behavior, 3*(24), 369–387.

Wang, M. T., & Eccles, J. S. (2012). Social support matters: Longitudinal effects of social support on three dimensions of school engagement from middle to high school. *Child Development, 83*(3), 877–895. Retrieved from http://www.ncbi.nlm.nih.gov/pubmed/22506836

Weiston-Serdan, T. (2015). *Critical mentoring: A definition and agenda.* Retrieved from https://wordpress.com/post/62521172/221/

Wolf, A. M., Del Prado Lippman, A., Glesmann, C., & Castro, E. (2015). *Process evaluation for the Office of Neighborhood Safety.* Retrieved from http://www.nccdglobal.org/sites/default/files/publication_pdf/ons-process-evaluation.pdf

Weiston-Serdan, T., & Vassor, S. (2016). In *Emerging voices in mentoring: Advancing a critical youth mentoring agenda.* Conference proceedings of the National Mentoring Summit, Washington, DC.

White House. (2014). *My Brother's Keeper initiative.* Retrieved from https://www.whitehouse.gov/my-brothers-keeper

Who are we? (n.d.). Retrieved from http://byp100.org/about/

Yoshino, K. (2007). *Covering: The hidden assault on our civil rights.* New York, NY: Random House.

INDEX

#BlackLivesMatter, 24–25, 94

AAMP. *See* African American
    Mentoring Program
academics
    culture enriched by, 46–47
    youth mentoring enriching, 38
action
    call to, 81–95
    of communities, 10, 45
    for culturally relevant practice,
        45–46
    for data collection, 77–79
    for LGBTQQ youth mentoring,
        60
    for youth centrism, 31–32
    for youth mentoring, 19–20
African American Mentoring
    Program (AAMP), 22
age, race, sexuality and, 53–57
AI. *See* appreciative inquiry
air
    act of clearing, 5–6
    critical mentoring helping to clear,
        20, 83
    racism as water and, 12
    as young person context, 6
    youth mentoring clearing, 6, 9

appreciative inquiry (AI), 66–68, 76

Baldwin, James, 57
Berardi, L., 10–11
Big Brothers of America, 7, 17
Black Youth Project, 24, 25
Boggan, DeVone, 32

Carmichael, Stokely, 24
Children's Crusade, 24
Cohen, Cathy, 25, 76
colonial settler approach, 43, 44, 45
Colon-Torres, Y., 10–11
community. *See also* community
    programs
    actions of, 10, 45
    collecting culturally relevant data
        in, 65–80
    critical mentoring transforming,
        18, 41, 81, 82
    CRT in marginalized, 12
    data shared with, 78–79
    definition of, 74–75
    empowerment evaluation
        including, 73
    engagement with, 32, 44, 47,
        84–85
    inclusion and partnership in, 26

liaisons of, 32–33
marginalization in, 8, 12, 14, 17,
    19, 26, 28, 36, 43, 44
mentors as critical in, 41
organizations transforming, 82
problems in, 9
racialization in, 8
schools partnering with, 88
volunteerism lacking in, 44
youth centrism in, 84
youth mentoring served by
    networks in, 8
community programs
    critical mentoring for, 83–85
    Cultural Mistrust Inventory
        helping mentors adjust, 11
    funding for, 18
    language of, 10
    opportunities for, 84
    planning and implementation of,
        21, 28
    responsibility of, 85
    working together of, 84
    young people partnering with,
        27–29, 33, 38
counternarratives
    challenges of, 61–62
    marginalized youth perspectives
        as, 13
    youth mentoring informed by, 16
Crenshaw, Kimberle, 52–53
critical consciousness
    concept of, 38
    critical mentoring triggering, 1–2
    cultural competence, academic
        success and, 37
    culturally relevant pedagogy as
        part of, 37–38
    culturally relevant practice
        connected to, 41, 47
    youth mentoring augmented by, 1

critical mentoring
    clearing the air helped by, 20, 83
    as collaborative, 82
    for colleges and universities,
        88–91
    communities transformed by, 18,
        41, 81, 82
    for community programs, 83–85
    concept of, 2, 41
    conversation yielded by, 17
    critical consciousness triggered
        by, 1–2
    CRT informing, 2, 14–17
    about cultural relevance, 46
    without deficit base, 42
    empowerment evaluation needed
        by, 74
    engagement required for, 18–19,
        63, 75, 83, 92
    for everyone, 82–83
    as evolving concept, 95
    funding for, 65
    goal of, 20
    guideposts of, 27–28
    for K-12 schools, 85–88
    language and praxis opened with,
        21, 58
    for leaders, 92–93
    legitimizing of, 79
    as multiple adverse elements, 72
    as participatory, 26, 82
    in political context, 94
    questions on research in, 91–92
    for researchers, 91–92
    responsibility of, 20, 86
    in schools, 87
    shifting to, 17–19
    systems changed by, 43
    transitioning to, 42–43
    water purified by, 20, 83
    work getting done for, 93

of students already live lives that break the gender binary and contest what Nicolazzo calls 'compulsory heterogenderism.' We owe it to those students to acknowledge their reality, and reflect it in our pedagogy, curriculum, and institutional practices."—**Susan Stryker**, *Associate Professor of Gender and Women's Studies, University of Arizona, and founding coeditor* of TSQ: Transgender Studies Quarterly

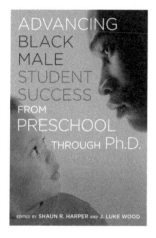

Advancing Black Male Student Success From Preschool Through Ph.D.

Edited by Shaun R. Harper and J. Luke Wood

"This book provides practical approaches for educators, parents, policymakers, and others who are committed to improving Black male student achievement. Instead of simply documenting challenges boys of color face, authors focus on proven structures, programs, and initiatives we can build upon. This is required reading for anyone committed to bringing out the genius in our youth."—**Jonathan Foy**, *Principal, Eagle Academy for Young Men, Bronx, New York Campus*

"*Advancing Black Male Student Success From Preschool Through Ph.D.* is a timely compendium that fruitfully contributes to the national conversation regarding the education of Black boys and men. Drawing on relevant research, best practices, and solid policy analyses, authors point the way to proven ideas and interventions that truly work throughout the educational pipeline. Morehouse College and many others will benefit from this text."—**John Silvanus Wilson Jr.**, *President, Morehouse College*

22883 Quicksilver Drive
Sterling, VA 20166-2102

Subscribe to our e-mail alerts: www.Styluspub.com

Also available from Stylus

Developing Effective Student Peer Mentoring Programs
A Practitioner's Guide to Program Design, Delivery, Evaluation, and Training

Peter J. Collier
Foreword by Nora Domínguez

"*Developing Effective Student Peer Mentoring Programs* is a superb book that should be read by all higher education professionals who are looking for practical strategies grounded in solid research to start a peer mentoring program. Peter Collier's book is an accessible comprehensive guide that provides specific approaches for serving veterans, international, and underrepresented students."—***Buffy Smith***, *University of St. Thomas, Minneapolis*

"Collier's treatment of peer mentorship is THE resource you want on this topic. It not only is grounded in theory and scholarship but also provides practical advice and institutional examples of peer mentor programs. It is comprehensive in its coverage of the history and purpose of these programs and also addresses the important elements of successful program delivery such as recruitment, training, and evaluation. Further, it is inclusive of peer mentoring for 'new-traditional' student populations such as international, service members and veterans, and first-generation undergraduates."—***Jennifer R. Keup***, *Director, National Resource Center for the First-Year Experience and Students in Transition*

Trans* in College
Transgender Students' Strategies for Navigating Campus Life and the Institutional Politics of Inclusion

Z Nicolazzo
Foreword by Kristen A. Renn
Afterword by Stephen John Quaye

"With recent estimates of the trans* population in the United States showing three to six times as many trans* people under the age of 18 as there are over the age of 18, the work Z Nicolazzo undertakes in this book should be required reading for educators at every level of instruction. Gender is changing in ways we can scarcely comprehend, and millions

(Continued on previous page)